# INTEGRATING THE
# 12 STEPS
## INTO
# ADDICTION
# THERAPY

# INTEGRATING THE
# 12 STEPS
# INTO
# ADDICTION
# THERAPY

## A Resource Collection and
## Guide for Promoting Recovery

## James R. Finley

**WILEY**

John Wiley & Sons, Inc.

---

**Note about Photocopy Rights**
The publisher grants purchasers permission to reproduce handouts from this book for professional use with their clients.

---

*Library of Congress Cataloging-in-Publication Data:*

Finley, James R., 1948–.
   Integrating the 12 steps into addiction therapy : a resource collection and
guide for promoting recovery / James R. Finley.
      p.   cm.
   Includes bibliographical references.
   ISBN 0-471-59980-8 (paper/cd-rom)
      1. Substance abuse—Treatment.   2. Twelve-step programs. I. Title:
Integrating the twelve-steps into addiction therapy. II. Title.
   RC564.F564      2004
   616.86′06—dc22

                                                                    2004005521

Printed in the United States of America.

10  9  8  7  6  5  4  3  2

*To Jan, my wife;*
*to Bill and David, my brothers;*
*to Chris and Jessica, my children;*
*and to Phillip and Matthew, my grandchildren;*
*with thanks for what we all give to one another;*
*and to the loving memory of my parents, Carol and George,*
*who showed us how.*

# CONTENTS

# PREFACE

Therapists, counselors, social workers, psychologists, psychiatrists, and other professionals working in the field of addiction treatment have taken a range of approaches to 12-step programs over the past several decades. A non-alcoholic physician who specialized in treating alcoholics, Dr. William Silkworth, was instrumental in the creation of Alcoholics Anonymous (AA) in 1935. Nearly 50 years ago, the American Medical Association (AMA) established a definition of alcoholism as a disease, later extending this to include other forms of chemical dependence. During the decades since the founding of AA, some clinicians have relied on 12-step programs as a cornerstone of treatment, while others have advocated other approaches and at times fiercely criticized the 12-step approach.

The arguments of both sides of this debate are examined in Section I of this book. However, aside from the discussion of the pros and cons of AA and related programs, the context of the debate and the treatment field has shifted in the era of managed care. Treatment is expected to be briefer, less intensive, and less expensive, and aftercare is harder to find or fund. Behavior is now the primary focus of therapy, as evidenced by the common replacement of the term *mental health* with *behavioral health.*

In today's world, the 12-step model is more valuable and necessary than ever before. Consistent with the emphasis on behavioral change, one of the many slogans often used in AA and its descendant programs is "you don't think your way into right acting, you act your way into right thinking." The foundation principles of 12-step life are honesty, open-mindedness, and willingness. These are non-addictive patterns of behavior and cognitive functioning that if learned and practiced will make the addict or alcoholic more open and receptive to other treatment interventions. They will also bring improvement in other behavioral problems that accompany addiction. They are often the treatment goals when dealing with marital and family relationship dysfunction and antisocial behavior.

The intent of this book is to provide clear explanations and practical tools for clinicians who are considering integrating 12-step participation into their work with their clients or patients and who want to learn more. It is also for those who are already using AA or other programs as resources and who are seeking tools and resources in a ready-to-use form easily adapted to meet the needs of a particular client or situation.

## HOW TO USE THIS BOOK

This book is organized into three sections and two appendices. The first section contains general information and guidelines on integrating treatment with 12-step work. The second section consists of 27 therapeutic homework assignments pertaining specifically to 12-step work, and the third section contains eight lesson plans for psychoeducational groups on topics related to 12-step work in early recovery. Appendix A is a partial list of recommended books and films for professional reference, self-education, and bibliotherapy or videotherapy, and Appendix B consists of the 12 Steps and 12 Traditions with notes on adaptations made by various 12-step programs addressing different addictive problems.

You may use the enclosed CD-ROM to install the homework assignments and lesson plans in a directory on your computer as Microsoft Word document files and Microsoft PowerPoint® presentation files, allowing you to customize them by rewording items, adding a logo or other art, or however else you choose. For further instructions, see the "About the CD-ROM" section.

If you have suggestions for improvement, or want to tell me about features you find especially useful, please contact me through John Wiley & Sons. As with previous volumes, I am grateful for whatever feedback you can give me.

JAMES R. FINLEY

**Section I**

# WHAT TO DO AND EXPECT (AND WHAT NOT TO DO)

## WHY INTEGRATE 12-STEP WORK INTO ADDICTION TREATMENT?

For decades, clinicians have argued both for and against the integration of 12-step work into addiction treatment. Here are some of the pros and cons of using the 12-step model in combination with other approaches.

### Cons

The role and efficacy of Alcoholics Anonymous (AA) and other 12-step addiction recovery programs have always been controversial in the addiction treatment community. Many clinicians have criticized these programs for several reasons, including:

- **Lack of Scientific Rigor**

  The 12-step model was created by nonprofessionals, who worked out their methodology by trial and error. The only element based on any medical or psychological theory was their insistence that alcoholism (and later other addictions) resulted from a disease process rather than being a matter of character or will power. When AA formed, this theory was held by a few pioneering physicians but still 20 years away from popular acceptance and was, in fact, rejected at the time by the American Medical Association.

  Further, since its origins, the structure and principles of the 12-step model have not easily lent themselves to research. The insistence on lack of affiliation with other organizations or institutions and the staunch protection of individual anonymity have made it very difficult for researchers to study the results of participation in these 12-step programs without the active support or involvement of the programs themselves.

- **Spiritual Orientation**

  The 12-step model explicitly states that recovery from addiction requires a relationship with a God or some type of Higher Power (i.e., an intangible and supernatural entity or force). It also insists that there is no one correct version of this God or Higher Power and that each member is responsible for coming to his or her own individual understanding of this being or power.

This is very difficult to accept, both for those who see no place for the mystical in modern medicine and therapy and for those who hold to a specific set of religious beliefs and reject the lack of a definitive doctrine regarding God.

Some object to the fact that although the 12-step model insists that it does not prescribe any particular brand of faith, much of the early literature frames its discussion of a Higher Power in terms of a masculine and Christian God, and many groups use specifically Christian prayers such as the Lord's Prayer as part of their meeting format.

- **Lack of Cooperation with Treatment Providers**

  AA and the other 12-step programs have a long-standing tradition of refraining from endorsing or affiliating themselves with outside organizations and/or institutions. As a result of this tradition, 12-step programs only offer partial treatment support. This support is usually limited to the following:

  - 12-step groups welcome people who are undergoing addiction treatment;

  - Meeting chairpersons will usually sign attendance sheets;

  - 12-step programs will bring meetings into treatment facilities; and

  - The 12-step programs provide information to professionals, through literature and in many communities via a 12-step program member designated as the Cooperation with the Professional Community (CPC) liaison.

  The programs will not assist with other treatment program activities or policies.

  Further, many members of the various 12-step programs have the mistaken belief that 12-step work and treatment don't mix. Many individuals in 12-step programs disparage outside treatment, although the official stance of the 12-step programs is that treatment and psychiatry are also valuable and sometimes necessary for recovery. Many other 12-step members express gratitude for the outside treatment programs through which they first got clean and sober.

**Pros**

Why is it a good idea for addiction treatment providers and programs to integrate participation in 12-step work with the services they offer their clients or patients? There are several compelling reasons, including:

- **Proven Effectiveness**
  Alcoholics Anonymous was founded in 1935, and in the decades since, many other recovery programs based on the AA model have been formed. More people have succeeded in achieving long-term recovery through AA and the other 12-step programs than by any other means. Many succeed in these programs after repeatedly failing to sustain recovery any other way, a common enough phenomenon that a 12-step program is typically referred to as "the last house on the street," meaning that all other options have failed.

  Although the majority of people who try AA do relapse and drift away, the long-term success rate of the 12-step programs still appears to be the best available. Also, when 12-step participation is sustained over a period of months as part of integration with treatment or relapse prevention programs, the proportion of people who continue to participate in the 12-step program and stay clean and sober rises significantly.

- **Knowledgeable Peer Role Modeling and Feedback**
  People who are new to recovery, or trying to begin recovery, find more positive examples and mentors in AA and other 12-step programs than in any other milieu. At each meeting, in sponsorship and in informal conversations outside of meetings, the new person is able to watch and listen as experienced peers use the tools of 12-step recovery to stay clean and sober and cope with life's challenges. Sponsors and others experienced in recovery offer valuable feedback and suggestions regarding the newcomer's interpretation and use of the 12 steps and the principles of these recovery programs.

- **Availability of Meetings between Treatment Sessions**
  Particularly with larger programs such as AA, Narcotics Anonymous (NA), and Overeaters Anonymous (OA), newly recovering

people can attend several meetings per week in many communities. This provides an opportunity for the recently clean and sober person to receive frequent reinforcement and maintain recovery as a priority in daily life, more so than if he/she is seeing a clinician only once or twice a week.

- **Healthy and Supportive Social Environment**
One of the greatest risk factors for relapse in people completing treatment is the negative influence of returning to an unchanged social environment where substance abuse may be a norm. In a 12-step program, the newly recovering person finds an alternative social network and often a calendar of addiction-free recreational activities such as sober dances, picnics, and parties. On a daily basis, he or she is surrounded by other recovering people in a subculture where sobriety is the standard.

- **Lifelong Aftercare**
A 12-step program also offers a framework for lifelong aftercare that is otherwise sorely lacking in many programs. Research has shown the importance of long-term interventions in bringing about long-term abstinence from addictive behaviors, but most treatment programs are limited to a few months at most. By integrating 12-step participation during that treatment period and getting the client or patient "rooted" in AA, NA, or another related program, the clinician can lay the groundwork for a lifelong self-managed program of aftercare. Many members of 12-step groups achieve decades of recovery and die sober.

- **Availability of Books, Workshops, and Tapes**
Literature is one of the primary tools used by 12-step programs since the inception of AA. These books are often found in mainstream bookstores. Larger communities often have recovery-oriented bookstores. Other vendors offer these products via the Internet. Most meetings sell the primary books used by their programs at wholesale prices without any markup, and often more experienced members buy books for newcomers who can't afford them. A trip to a bookstore will yield a variety of books and workbooks for going through the steps.

In most parts of the country there are frequent workshops, conventions, and other events centered on 12-step recovery in various programs. Many meeting places post information about these events on bulletin boards.

Both in recovery bookstores and at workshops and conventions, audiotapes and sometimes videotapes are available, usually recordings of speakers making presentations on various topics at previous gatherings.

There are many Internet web sites devoted to 12-step recovery, offering online literature, chat room meetings, and directories and calendars of events. Many recovery-oriented bookstores have web sites where people can buy literature and even jewelry, T-shirts, and similar items.

All of these resources can be effective adjuncts to treatment through bibliotherapy assignments between sessions, in guided discussions in treatment groups, and as useful background reading for clinicians seeking to improve their own expertise.

- **Holistic Approach**
Although the design of the 12-step model and the traditional practices of groups using this model were developed through trial and error, they have evolved to effectively model multiple therapeutic approaches to both addictions and other life problems.

The sharing that takes place in meetings and between individuals can be a powerful psychodynamic intervention, as people relive formative experiences to gain insight, express previously withheld emotions, and find validation and acceptance from others with similar experiences.

The process of working through the steps themselves involves intense cognitive work as the recovering person reviews past and current patterns of thought and behavior, identifies errors and distortions in his or her thinking, replaces them with more functional patterns of cognition, and establishes a daily routine to maintain self-awareness and self-correction when distortion creeps back into thought patterns.

The many actions included in the steps and in the norms and common practices in 12-step groups act as effective behavioral interventions, replacing self-destructive habits and coping strategies with healthier ones.

Finally, the acceptance and encouragement 12-step groups provide their members is a potent source of the unconditional positive regard emphasized in humanistic approaches to treatment.

- **Specialized 12-Step Programs for Many Problems**
  Any clinician is likely to encounter clients with addictive problems for which no specialized treatment program is accessible. In many situations, there may be no way to get clients into psychotherapeutic programs even for chemical dependencies. Often, a 12-step group that can fill this gap will be available to the client or patient, either locally or via electronic chat room meetings on the Internet. These can provide vital adjuncts to individual therapy or counseling. Where the specialized treatment programs needed are available, the corresponding 12-step programs can be useful to reinforce those programs and provide aftercare.

- **No Cost or Time Limitations**
  Finally, at a time when funding for treatment is stretched more every year and clients or patients may be in more and more difficult financial situations, the 12-step programs are free of any cost. In each meeting, a collection is taken up, but contribution is completely voluntary, and many members are indeed unable to chip in. No distinctions are made between those who can afford to put money in the basket and those who can't. Even those who can afford to do more usually contribute only a dollar or two per meeting.

## Conclusion

Twelve-step groups can be a valuable tool for clinicians by augmenting the work done in treatment and by filling gaps to meet particular client needs, such as daily reinforcement, a positive peer culture, and long-term aftercare, when there may be no other way to provide these things. For clinicians using an informed approach, the inclusion of this valuable and widely available set of resources in treatment planning and delivery offers benefits that far outweigh the liabilities. Counselors, therapists, social workers, psychologists, and physicians working with addictions can become more effective by learning about 12-step programs and integrating their use into their array of other treatment modalities.

Many clinicians approach 12-step programs with trepidation because they are concerned about making mistakes relative to the traditions and practices of these programs that might reduce their credibility or alienate clients. The simple guidelines in this book help avoid errors in working with clients who are participating in 12-step programs as part of their treatment regimen.

## ANONYMITY AND CONFIDENTIALITY

As implied by the word "anonymous" in the name of every 12-step program, the framework of the 12-step program includes a strong tradition of mutual protection of identity. The tradition of anonymity also means that members are expected to refrain from identifying themselves as belonging to any 12-step program in any medium likely to be exposed to a mass audience. No member of a 12-step program should identify any other member without the other member's specific consent. Regardless of consent, no 12-step program participant should ever be identified in the mass media. This applies to both members' names and any identifiable images and includes print and electronic media.

The tradition of anonymity also extends to the confidences revealed by others in 12-step meetings. This anonymity is critical to using the 12-step approach.

In practical terms, this means that no clinician should ever ask a client to:

1.  Identify another member of a 12-step program.

2.  Publicly identify himself or herself as a program participant.

3.  Report on what someone else said or did in a 12-step meeting in a way that would reveal the identity of that other person.

In fact, if a client reports or indicates his or her intent to do any of these things, the clinician should remind the client of the program traditions and advise him or her to consult with a sponsor or other experienced 12-step mentor before taking the action.

Clients who are participants in 12-step programs may:

1.  Voluntarily identify themselves as such in individual conversations.

2. Talk about things they have heard in 12-step meetings, provided they don't include names or identifying details of what was shared.

3. Anonymously provide information about their own 12-step experiences for use in mass media or documentaries.

4. Publicly identify themselves as being in recovery from their addiction, without mentioning that they are participating in a 12-step program.

## ENSURING THAT CLIENTS ARE PARTICIPATING EFFECTIVELY IN 12-STEP ACTIVITIES

As part of the disease, the typical client in treatment for addiction is likely to be resistant to therapeutic strategies and activities, and to be dishonest about his or her activities related to the addiction. This means that treatment often includes means to check and verify that the client is complying with the treatment plan, such as a requirement that he or she submit to random drug screenings.

When a client is participating in 12-step programs, the most commonly used means of confirming attendance is a signature sheet, which the client is required to have signed by the person chairing each meeting he or she attends. This tool sometimes works but just as often fails when the client engaging in one or more resistant behaviors, such as:

1. He or she may avoid the meetings and forge signatures or initials on the signature sheet.

2. The client may arrive early, get the sheet signed, and leave a few minutes into the meeting, or show up during the last few minutes and get the sheet signed at the end.

3. Finally, the client may be physically present in the meeting place, but either ignore what is being said or spend the majority of the time taking breaks to smoke outside, drink coffee, and engage in other activities that prevent his or her actually attending to the meeting's content.

For these reasons, the clinician may wish to pursue other strategies to ensure the client's participation in the 12-step program. You may choose to use the *12-Step Meeting/Critique Form* exercise from this book, which avoids violating 12-step traditions regarding anonymity but requires the client to report specifics about the content of a meeting and about the client's cognitive and emotional responses. If the clinician has taken the time to attend a few open 12-step meetings to get a feel for how the meetings flow and what a typical meeting is like, it will be difficult for a client who is not attending or paying attention to deceive his or her counselor or therapist.

A less formal tactic is to simply engage the client in conversations using probing questions along the lines of those included in the exercise mentioned, as well as to ask the client to describe other 12-step work he or she is doing with a 12-step sponsor. No experienced 12-step sponsor is likely to allow a sponsee (a person being sponsored) to avoid frequent participation in meetings, and most sponsors ask that their sponsees accompany them to meetings. Some sponsors are willing to talk with clinicians and confirm a client's participation in the 12-step program.

## HELPING CLIENTS BENEFIT FROM THEIR 12-STEP PROGRAMS

The clinician should look for opportunities for mutual reinforcement among the 12-step work and the other treatment modalities being used. For treatment programs that are heavily *behavioral,* it can be useful to focus the client on the specific changes in behavior that are practiced and described by a sponsor and other role models who have achieved long-term recovery. This is described as "changing playpens and playmates," that is, avoiding places and situations in which the client formerly practiced his or her addiction and replacing the old social network with a support system of recovering people. Other behavioral strategies normally advocated in 12-step programs include:

- Daily attendance at meetings.

- Making a commitment to call a sponsor or another person in recovery before acting on an urge to relapse.

- Engaging in morning and evening prayer and/or meditation.

- The activities involved in carrying out the 12 steps themselves.

## CASE STUDY

For John, an experienced addictions counselor, Diane was the most frustrating client on his caseload. John felt that their therapeutic rapport was good, but he had tried every behavioral intervention and tactic he knew and she kept relapsing. Diane seemed sincere in her distress at each loss of control and vowed once again to be stronger next time and to do the behavioral homework assignments John gave her, but he had ceased to be surprised when she came in to sessions sweating and shaky, sometimes still under the influence, and with her homework undone. Somehow she had forgotten or been unable to follow through on her plans when the craving for a drink hit her, as it did every day near the time she got off work.

John and Diane had talked several times about the prospect of her participating in Alcoholics Anonymous. Each time she had refused, giving reasons ranging from a dislike of religion to a fear of talking in front of people. Finally John told Diane that he couldn't think of anything else they hadn't tried, and that he was going to add participation in AA to her treatment plan. He told her that if she was unwilling to try it, he would refer her to another therapist but would not continue to work with her, since working with him appeared to be providing her with little or no therapeutic benefit.

Diane reluctantly agreed to try it. With her input and concurrence, John drew up an addition to her treatment plan calling for her to begin attending a meeting near her workplace that started just after her workday ended, starting that day, and to attend at least one meeting per day for two weeks. For each meeting Diane attended, she was to complete a 12-step meeting review and critique form. In addition to going to meetings, the treatment plan called for Diane to choose a sponsor from among the women she met in this group before her next session with John.

At their next session on Monday, Diane greeted John with a storm of complaints about the new assignments. The meetings were stupid and boring; she had nothing in common with the others there; all they did was talk about God and make corny jokes; they didn't understand her problems. She hadn't asked anyone to sponsor her. And Diane had relapsed again over the weekend.

John responded by reminding her of her promise to get a sponsor and asked to see her meeting review forms. Diane had only completed two forms. After examining them, John suspected that she had filled them out in haste just before their session rather than after the meetings. He asked her to read through the forms with him, expanding on her answers. He pointed out that she had stayed sober for four days before relapsing, which was an improvement. Before the session ended, John and Diane signed a written contract in which she agreed to arrive at least 10 minutes before the AA meeting each day, say hello to one woman she hadn't talked with before, stay 10 minutes after the end of the meeting, and take a different route home from work that didn't take her past her favorite bar. She also agreed in writing to ask another woman to be at least a temporary sponsor before the next meeting.

Week by week John continued to work with Diane, reinforcing her behavior when she attended meetings, made new friendships there, asked an older woman named Barb to be her sponsor, and began having weeks without relapses. After the first two weeks, they agreed to renew this portion of her treatment plan for another two weeks. When Diane reported that Barb had threatened to fire her as a sponsee unless she started working the 12 steps, John provided her with handouts giving her formats for each step in turn, which she used with Barb.

After six weeks, Diane reported that she had started noticing that others were talking about experiences she could relate to, especially in the way they felt. She reported spending more time socializing with her new friends in AA and finding that calling Barb or going to a meeting when she felt the urge to drink helped her avoid acting on the impulse until it had passed. She was starting to feel better physically and was becoming more productive at work.

As time passed, Diane found her daily behaviors changing more and more under the influence of her therapeutic homework assignments and her new circle of acquaintances in AA, particularly Barb. During the same session in which Diane showed John the 30-day sobriety chip she had received at her group's monthly birthday meeting, she told him that she thought she might continue attending the meetings even when she was done with therapy because she was comfortable with the people there and they were good to her.

For cognitive and cognitive-behavioral orientations, useful synergy with a 12-step program can be achieved by focusing on how the 12-step work helps the client identify and change habitual distortions in his or her thinking. Specific patterns that are highlighted and targeted in 12-step activities and literature include resentment, self-pity, and rationalization. By exploring this part of the 12-step work with the client in session, the clinician can strengthen and reinforce the effects of the positive peer culture in the groups. Another aspect of 12-step work that is particularly useful from a cognitive-behavioral perspective is its emphasis on introspection and self-analysis of motives, guiding the client to insight regarding the role of his or her fears and insecurities in much of the dysfunctional behavior associated with addictions.

## CASE STUDY

Carol had been in practice for three years, and felt she was hitting her stride. Her theoretical orientation was cognitive-behavioral, and she had been pleased with the results this approach yielded with most of her clients. David, however, was different. With all the interventions she had tried so far to help him overcome his gambling addiction, he had clearly "gotten it" in terms of recognizing the distortions in his own thinking and the resulting negative consequences in his life. In other areas, he had made strides in changing his cognitive patterns and resulting behavior. When it came to the slot machines, though, David seemed to leave his insights behind when he left Carol's office. Now he was facing financial disaster and the prospect of going to jail for violating the terms of the probation to which he had been assigned after writing a number of bad checks to finance a spree at the casino.

In a case conference, Carol's supervisor suggested that she try assigning David to attend Gamblers Anonymous (GA) meetings. Carol's graduate school program hadn't spent much time on addictions, especially nonchemical addictions, and hadn't mentioned 12-step programs, so she attended an open meeting at a local club and read a book containing personal accounts of GA members. She was impressed with the openness and mutual support she saw and read about. At their next session, Carol told David she wanted to add participation in the GA program to his treatment plan.

David wasn't enthusiastic, but agreed that he had little to lose. They worked out a plan in which he would attend meetings three times a week, all that was possible in that community. Guided by her supervisor, Carol also asked David to read the same book she had just read and to choose another man as a temporary sponsor during his first week and make a commitment to call this sponsor every day and whenever he felt urges to gamble. They made a written contract in which David committed himself to follow through on these actions, and Carol gave him a signature sheet to take to meetings.

After three weeks, Carol noticed that although David appeared enthusiastic about his activity in GA and was using the jargon of the program in their conversations, his patterns of thought and behavior didn't seem to be changing. Taking a closer look at the signature sheet he had been bringing to his sessions, she noted that the handwriting in the signatures or initials for many of the days was suspiciously similar to that in David's initials on the pages of his treatment plan. She confronted him. David at first insisted that he had been going to meetings, but when Carol began probing him with questions taken from a meeting review and critique form, he admitted that he had only gone to three meetings and had left early, that he hadn't really found a sponsor, and that despite his attempts to control his behavior with willpower he had gambled several times.

Carol used the situation as a teaching moment with David, discussing the role of deception in addictive behavior and the cognitive dissonance he was experiencing with his professed value system. He agreed that he sincerely wanted to quit for good and was willing to do whatever it took.

Carol and David drew up a new contract in which David agreed not only to attend the meetings he was supposed to be going to, but to find a sponsor who was willing to let David give Carol his first name only and was willing to talk with Carol on the telephone and confirm David's participation in GA activities. The new contract also included a timetable in which David agreed to work the first five steps during the next two weeks with his sponsor, using handouts Carol provided for each step.

During the next two sessions, Carol noted that David was becoming less evasive and admitted to some self-destructive and criminal behaviors he had never told her about before. As he worked Steps 4 and 5, David began to talk in terms of his own accountability for his actions and, more importantly, about how he was changing his ways of interacting with others, including his probation officer. She noted that his self-perception was shifting from seeing himself as a perpetual victim to perceiving himself as increasingly empowered.

As David continued through the steps, he ran into some difficulties and resistance with Step 9, the step concerned with making restitution to others he had harmed. He was afraid that if he went to face some of the people he had lied to or stolen from, he might end up being either locked up or killed; and yet his sponsor insisted that this was necessary. Together David and his sponsor worked out a plan to make some amends anonymously in cases where people didn't realize what David had done or it would be unsafe to approach them. With others, David and Carol met with his probation officer (PO) and explained that he was trying to work the 12 steps thoroughly but feared incarceration if he revealed some of his secrets. His PO told them that he had been impressed with the changes he was seeing in David, and that if the crimes about which David was concerned had taken place before he began his GA activity, he would not hold them against him as long as he stayed out of trouble from that point on. David went on to work Step 9 and reported another positive shift in his self-perception as a result. As he went on to incorporate Steps 10 through 12 into his daily life, David's old patterns of self-deception, rationalization, and minimization continued to diminish and he grew more and more open to self-examination, often spotting and correcting his own cognitive distortions between sessions and simply reporting the results to Carol. Gradually his finances improved. Ultimately he successfully terminated treatment and later completed his probation without incident.

---

From a psychodynamic or existential stance, 12-step work can be most useful when the client is engaged in reexamining past losses and traumas and concerns about the meaning and worth of his or her existence. He or she may never have processed these concerns emotionally and may have been using the addiction to avoid facing them. A common experience reported by many newly recovering alcoholics and addicts is that of being overwhelmed by feelings of anger, grief, and fear. They have used their addiction as an emotional anesthetic to avoid confronting these feelings. A common joke in 12-step meetings is that the word *sober* is an acronym for "son of a bitch, everything's real!" The psychodynamic approach also ties in well with the reexperiencing, reinterpretation, and resolution of difficult life experiences that is associated with Steps 4, 5, 8, and 9.

---

## CASE STUDY

Don was a fascinating but frustrating client. He had once had a dangerous drinking problem and had quit drinking only to begin abusing prescribed pain medications. Mike, an Employee Assistance Program (EAP) therapist to whom Don had come at his supervisor's insistence after he had failed a random drug test, had worked with addicts before. But unlike others who had been able to change their behavior when its consequences got painful enough, Don seemed unable to quit no matter what. Now he was facing the possibility of divorce, and the risk of losing his job if he failed another drug screening at work, and he was still using drugs.

Don always presented as cheerful and tended to joke about his difficulties, though once in a while the façade would slip and he would look scared and tired. He tended to evade discussion of painful experiences past and present, and he had a history of turning to absorbing experiences as well as alcohol to cope with uncomfortable feelings. At different times, he had become deeply involved with various hobbies and at other times, engaged in workaholic behavior. Don seemed quite self-assured, often trying hard to impress others, and Mike's impression was that Don was trying to prove something to himself but was never quite convinced. All Mike's efforts to get past Don's front and get him to examine his painful childhood, his failing marriage, or his inability to sit still with his emotions were skillfully deflected.

One day Don appeared for his session looking excited. He told Mike that he'd run into a friend who had formerly had a severe pill problem but had apparently overcome it. His friend, Tommy, had given Don some literature about Narcotics Anonymous. Don wanted to try NA and see whether it would help him. He had been to a meeting and had been impressed by the fact that the people there had been laughing and joking about their past drug problems. Grateful for a new tack to try, Mike amended Don's treatment plan to include some psychodynamic interventions making use of the NA program and Don set out to put them into application. These included going to meetings, reading the book titled *Narcotics Anonymous,* and asking his friend Tommy to be his temporary sponsor.

Don came to his next session shaken and crestfallen. He reported that NA was not the lighthearted organization he'd taken it for. At a meeting he'd heard a woman sharing about a recent relapse that had resulted in a trip to the emergency room, her husband leaving her and taking their children, and her probation officer scheduling a hearing to consider incarcerating her; the woman had broken down and begun crying. Don had identified strongly with her feelings and had found himself also beginning to cry. He had left the meeting early and hadn't been back, though he was still talking with Tommy.

Mike dedicated the first part of the session to walking Don through the first step, using a detailed written format and examining his helplessness to control his own drug use and his fear of where it would take him. During the second part, they went on to Step 2. Don was initially resistant to talking about God, having a long-standing antipathy to organized religion, but when Mike pointed out that the step only asked him to admit that it was *possible* a God of some kind *might* be able to help him, Don was able to accept the idea and left the session feeling more hopeful. His parting assignment was to go back to the meetings and to review his work on the first two steps with his sponsor, Tommy, and go on to Step 3.

As the next few weeks proceeded, Tommy took Don through Steps 3 through 7, with Mike monitoring his progress and discussing Don's thoughts and feelings with him each week. It was a difficult period for Don. Working through the Fourth Step brought to the surface of his awareness the unresolved feelings resulting from many years of painful experiences, starting with a childhood marked by neglect and abuse. Don was a churning human volcano of anger, grief, and anxiety during this time, and Mike made sure that Don was staying close to Tommy and that Don had the ability to contact Mike in an emergency.

As this process continued, however, Don did stay clean, and began to display a wider range of emotions and perceptions in his sessions with Mike. He reported that he was also sharing much of what they talked about with Tommy. In many cases when he spoke during meetings, he was receiving validation, acceptance, and emotional support. When Don completed his Fifth Step with Tommy, he chose to share it with Mike as well, and reported feeling afterward that a great burden had been lifted from his shoulders. Don described becoming free of troubling thoughts and memories that had haunted him for many years and been barriers to intimacy with his wife. His wife, Kathy, had begun attending Nar-Anon meetings, and their communication was improving. Their marriage seemed much more likely to survive than it had a few weeks earlier.

Don continued to work the steps with Tommy and to share his experiences in NA with Mike for three months, the duration of his Employee Assistance Program (EAP) benefit. At the end of that time, he had worked all the steps, had made regular participation in NA a part of his lifestyle, and had become very active in 12-step service work, going to talk with addicts who called to seek help from NA, an activity that gave Don great satisfaction. He and his wife socialized regularly with friends from the local 12-step community. Don was still struggling with his feelings about his past, and Mike referred him to a therapist covered by his regular health insurance to continue his counseling.

---

For the clinician approaching treatment from a humanistic stance of unconditional positive regard, the 12-step emphasis on self-acceptance, presented as the positive side of humility and reinforced through Step 5 in particular, dovetails well with this approach.

---

## CASE STUDY

Carrie was meeting Roger, a new client, for the first time. Distinctly overweight and disheveled in his dress and grooming, he slouched in the chair beside her desk, studying his scuffed shoes and mumbling replies to her questions and comments. Carrie was struck by the dead quality of his affect. She would have noticed that he was severely depressed if he'd been a stranger on the subway. With the history she gathered and her observations in Roger's intake interview, Carrie came to a provisional diagnosis of major depressive disorder, severe without psychotic features, coupled with dysthymic disorder—double depression—accompanied by an eating disorder, which she coded as a mental disorder affecting simple obesity. In talking with Roger, she quickly noted a pattern of self-medication for painful emotions by eating foods high in simple carbohydrates. In his initial treatment plan, Carrie set out a program of cognitive-behavioral interventions and also referred Roger to the psychiatrist in her group practice to be evaluated for antidepressant medication.

In their second session, Carrie realized that a common thread running through Roger's depression and other problems was a devastatingly poor self-image and a great deal of shame, which had apparently started when he was a child. His parents had joined his siblings and the other children in his neighborhood in teasing Roger for being overweight and at home had put him on various diets and berated him about his size. As he had responded by withdrawing into isolation, he had been further shamed because of his deteriorating school performance and lack of friendships. As an adult, Roger had nothing positive or hopeful to say about himself. Carrie decided that a strong Rogerian focus would be helpful for Roger; and after talking it over with her supervisor, chose a strategy of combining this approach with an assignment for Roger to begin attending meetings of two 12-step programs, Overeaters Anonymous (OA) and Emotions Anonymous (EA). She worked to get Roger to open up, encouraging him to talk about himself and his life and giving him positive feedback, and asked him to tell her about his experiences as he began participating in OA and EA.

At first Roger wasn't very responsive and was noncompliant with anything Carrie asked him to do outside of their sessions. After the first couple of weeks of his therapy, as his antidepressant medication began working and he began to be more open in response to Carrie's feedback, he began going to OA and EA meetings regularly.

In the beginning, Roger had a hard time with both programs and with OA in particular. He felt that people were critical of him, that he wasn't accepted in the groups, and that he had little in common with the others he met there. Carrie congratulated Roger for sticking with it and encouraged him to do three things in both OA and EA:

1.  Talk in the meetings and in particular talk about the thoughts and feelings that were painful for him.

2.  Find a sponsor from among more experienced participants in each program.

3.  Go to the meetings 10 minutes early and stay 10 minutes late and talk with at least one person before and one person after each meeting.

Roger reported that when he shared his feelings with the groups, others paid attention to him, let him know that they had felt the same way, and encouraged him. He began to emerge from his social isolation, and as the weeks passed he began to gain more ability to manage both his eating and his moods.

The crisis came when Roger's OA sponsor, Jack, told him it was time to write his Step-4 inventory. Roger procrastinated for as long as he could, then set to work. He found himself sinking back into self-loathing and shame as he contemplated his own role in his many problems, and Carrie wondered whether she had steered him wrong. Her supervisor reassured her that this was a temporary phase.

Sure enough, two sessions later Roger came to Carrie's office somehow managing to look both elated and relaxed. He told her that he had done his OA Step 5, sharing his Step-4 inventory with Jack. He described how he had shaken with fear as he read aloud what he had written about his most shameful secrets, one after another, and then how Jack had merely smiled and told Roger that he, Jack, had thought, done, and felt many of the same things, and told Roger some of his own secrets that made Roger feel his own weren't so dark. Roger was now looking forward to working through these same steps with the fellow EA member he had chosen as a sponsor.

Carrie reflected that the unconditional acceptance and positive regard Roger had found in Jack was a marvelous complement to what she was working to give him in his therapy, and vice versa.

---

When the treatment approach is transpersonal or otherwise spiritually based, the 12-step model may be the best fit of all, with its nonsectarian emphasis on finding and relying on a relationship with a Higher Power of some kind.

---

## CASE STUDY

Larry, a self-admitted "credit card junkie," had tried working with several clinicians already but found that their view of things seemed to include no place for his spiritual questions, and the cognitive or psychodynamic approaches they tried with him seemed incomplete and didn't work for him. He told his new therapist, Cheryl, that he felt trapped between his antipathy toward all the churches he'd ever experienced and his yearning for some kind of spiritual practice in his life. This had led him to various New Age movements and groups, but they too had disappointed him. In the meantime, his spending was digging him into an ever-deeper hole.

Cheryl had a background in pastoral counseling and her first impulse was to suggest ways for Larry to integrate his spiritual quest with cognitive strategies to overcome his addictive spending. As they began their work, she also asked Larry to read a book about the Debtors Anonymous (DA) 12-step program and to attend half a dozen meetings during the first two weeks.

Larry was open to the other work Cheryl wanted him to do, but at first he was resistant to DA. There was a person in the local DA group who frequently announced that his Higher Power was the God of a specific church with which Larry had gone through a big disillusionment when the behavior of the minister and board failed to match the ideals they professed. Larry was also uncomfortable because the local group always ended meetings by saying the Lord's Prayer.

Cheryl persuaded Larry to keep going to the meetings by pointing out that he was hearing only one person's interpretation of the phrase "God as we understood God" in Steps 3 and 11. She assigned him the task of finding a DA sponsor before their next session. Once he had done so, Cheryl gave Larry the assignment of working through the first three steps with his sponsor, an elderly woman named Liz, using handouts she provided to give him a structured format for each step. She also assigned Larry the task of asking DA members who belonged to at least five different churches or faith communities about their understanding of a Higher Power.

Larry reported that when he talked with others, they had explained to him that no one in a 12-step group has any right to try to impose his or her understanding of a Higher Power on any other person, that there is no one way to look at this subject, and that he had found that there was indeed a wide variety of views. Larry also found that when he went through Step 3 with Liz, he experienced a relief from his preoccupation with debting that he had not been able to achieve before.

Taking her cue from this success, Cheryl began structuring Larry's treatment plan primarily around his DA participation, choosing interventions to supplement and reinforce his work on each step as he proceeded.

Over the weeks that followed, Larry was able to gain more control over his spending than he had ever managed before. He told Cheryl that it felt to him as if he hadn't done it so much as allowed it to happen. He had several experiences of powerful urges to spend money on luxury items he couldn't afford but was able to get past them both because he had gotten rid of all his credit cards and because he had made a commitment to Liz that he would call her before he spent any money on things other than housing expenses, groceries, and transportation. He contacted a financial counselor and put together a plan to restore his finances to a reasonable state over the next three years.

It seemed that, for Larry, the key to success was to rely on a direct relationship with a personally defined God "with no middleman," as he jokingly put it, in combination with practical cognitive and behavioral interventions.

---

For other theoretical models, as well as for eclectic approaches, the clinician may examine the process of working through the 12 steps and becoming a practicing member of the 12-step recovery community and find tie-ins between other therapeutic techniques and the client's step work wherever they appear to fit together most effectively. Any treatment approach will resonate with some portion of the 12-step recovery process.

## POSITIONS OF 12-STEP PROGRAMS ON PSYCHOTHERAPY AND MEDICATIONS

This issue is widely misunderstood even within the 12-step programs. Ignorance and misinterpretations of the official stance of the 12-step programs even by very experienced individuals in recovery groups have led to many instances of trauma and even tragedy, as others at meetings have urged people participating in psychotherapy or taking psychiatric or pain medications to give these things up, sometimes even telling them they could not consider themselves in recovery as long as they were taking medication of any kind.

Bill Wilson, one of the cofounders of Alcoholics Anonymous, suffered from severe depression and spent years in counseling. The Big Book of AA (*Alcoholics Anonymous,* 4th ed.) advises members as follows:

> But this does not mean that we disregard human health resources. God has abundantly supplied this world with fine doctors, psychologists, and practitioners of various kinds. Do not hesitate to take your health problems to such persons. Most of them give freely of themselves, that their fellows may enjoy sound minds and bodies. Try to remember that though God has wrought miracles among us, we should never belittle a good doctor or psychiatrist. Their services are often indispensable in treating a newcomer and in following his case afterward. (Alcoholics Anonymous, p. 133)

Other 12-step programs take similar positions. If a client finds that individuals in a meeting he or she attends advise otherwise, it may be useful to refer the client to this passage and to advise him or her to seek guidance from a local central office.

As for medications, the official position of Alcoholics Anonymous, which is mirrored by the other 12-step programs, holds that while members must be aware of their own tendencies to seek chemical "quick fixes" for physical and emotional pain, there are legitimate uses of medication. As long as a recovering person is dealing with a physician who understands addictions, has advised that physician of his or her status as an alcoholic or addict in recovery, and is taking the medications exactly as prescribed, the use of medications is not in conflict with sobriety. This is spelled out in a pamphlet published by Alcoholics Anonymous World Services, Inc., and approved by the Alcoholics Anonymous General Service Conference, titled *The A.A. Member—Medications and Other Drugs: A Report from a Group of Physicians in A.A.* This 22-page pamphlet relates the personal experiences of several AA members, both some who relapsed as the result of use of medications that did not meet the guidelines stated above and some who relapsed after attempting to maintain their sobriety (and in one case became suicidal) *without* their medications and found that the key to sobriety for them was the proper and responsible use of their prescribed medications. This pamphlet can be of immense value in working with clients facing this issue, and every clinician who works with people suffering from addictions should read it and keep a copy available to share with clients.

Another useful resource for clients with questions about the use of medications that may be necessary to treat mood, anxiety, or thought disorders is a Double Trouble group and/or an Emotions Anonymous group, if available in the client's community. Double Trouble is a 12-step program specifically intended for people suffering from both addictions and other mental or emotional illnesses; Emotions Anonymous is a 12-step program for people suffering from mood and anxiety disorders.

## THINGS 12-STEP PROGRAMS CAN AND CAN'T DO FOR CLIENTS

### Here Are Some Things a 12-Step Program Can Do for a Client in Treatment for Addiction:

- Provide confirmation of meeting attendance via signature sheet, at the client's request, unless a specific group has a policy of not doing this (some have such policies, but they are rare),

- Provide a positive peer culture to replace a negative peer group and social/recreational environment that encourages addictive behavior,

- Provide individual mentoring, and

- Provide free, indefinite, and widely available support and reinforcement for healthy behavior, via meetings, individual interactions, conventions and conferences, and in a crisis by telephone or in-person visits coordinated by a local central office.

### Here Are Some Things a 12-Step Program Cannot Do:

- Provide a clinician with information about the quality or content of a client's participation in 12-step activities,

- Provide detoxification services, medically supervised or otherwise,

- Provide support in terms of funding, housing, or employment, or

- Provide actual counseling or therapy.

In summary, 12-step work is not treatment or therapy in and of itself. It is a useful adjunct and follow-up, which both increases the likelihood of successful completion of treatment and serves as an excellent resource for indefinite aftercare.

## INCORPORATING 12-STEP WORK INTO TREATMENT PLANNING

As mentioned, 12-step work is not treatment or therapy in and of itself. Because of this, it is best incorporated into a treatment plan in combination with other activities in support of a common goal and objective.

A. Typical treatment goals or objectives supported by 12-step activities could include the following categories:

1. Cognitive/behavioral:

   a. Correct distorted perceptions and overcome denial about the severity and nature of the client's problem and his or her inability to control it without help.

   b. Learn and practice relapse prevention skills to become and remain abstinent from addictive behavior.

   c. Learn and practice effective coping skills for life stressors to reduce the perceived need for self-medication.

   d. Form more functional habits of thought and behavior to supplant dysfunctional and self-destructive patterns.

2. Psychodynamic:

   a. Reexperience and resolve traumatic life experiences in a supportive environment.

   b. Learn and practice effective means of expressing and resolving emotional distress.

3. Humanistic:

   a. Experience self-revelation and complete acceptance from a peer.

   b. Experience increased self-esteem as a result of being of service to others.

4. Transpersonal:
    a. Form a positive spiritual belief system.
    b. Learn and practice a spiritually based system of values.

B. Many organizations and third-party payers expect treatment plans to include measurement of progress on each goal or objective. Even when not required by others, the clinician needs this kind of measurement to evaluate the outcomes of treatment interventions. In the past, many clinicians tried to satisfy this requirement with quantitative reporting of activities. In the context of 12-step work, this would consist of reporting the number of meetings a client has attended or some similar measure. This is less likely to satisfy requirements for measurement than in past years because it doesn't give any information about the effects of the meetings on the client's behavior. It will be more effective to use outcome measures such as concrete changes in the client's behaviors not only in the area of substance use but also in his or her interactions with others; employment; basic self-care in terms of diet, sleep, and exercise; and financial management. Where these changes can be connected with the 12-step work done by the client, this should be noted in treatment updates and progress notes.

**Section II**

# HOMEWORK ASSIGNMENTS

Section II contains 27 therapeutic homework assignments related to 12-step work. These assignments are meant to augment treatment between sessions in outpatient, intensive outpatient, or inpatient models and to help the client progress more quickly in his or her 12-step work.

Depending on the theoretical orientation of the treatment regimen, the assignments may be presented as supplements to behavioral, cognitive-behavioral, psychodynamic, transpersonal, or eclectic therapeutic interventions. The assignments themselves are primarily cognitive in nature and combine the visual and tactile/kinesthetic learning modalities by requiring the client to read the assignment and write responses. In many cases, they employ auditory learning as well by tasking clients to consult with other members of 12-step groups and get their feedback.

If taken in order, the first five assignments help clients begin the process of 12-step recovery by guiding them through the first stages of understanding how these recovery programs work and affiliating with recovery groups and 12-step program sponsors, the mentors who will guide them in their ongoing step work.

The next 12 assignments walk the newly recovering client through the 12 steps themselves, providing a structured framework for the cognitive and behavioral requirements of each step.

Finally, the last 10 assignments cover relapse prevention in high-stress situations, use of 12-step literature, special issues for several specific client populations, and assistance for the client's family in understanding and supporting the recovery process.

# UNDERSTANDING SPIRITUALITY IN 12-STEP PROGRAMS

## GOALS OF THIS EXERCISE

1. Overcome resistance to participation in 12-step programs based on perceptions that they are religious in orientation.

2. Develop an understanding of the differences between religion and spirituality as practiced in 12-step programs.

3. Guide the client in aspects of early 12-step work that address questions of spirituality, in particular Steps 2 and 3.

## SUGGESTIONS FOR PROCESSING THIS EXERCISE WITH CLIENTS

This exercise is designed for newly recovering clients who are resistant to participating in 12-step programs because they are uncomfortable with religion for any reason. Its approach is to guide clients in thinking through definitions of the terms involved, analyzing the value and utility of the spiritual practices in 12-step programs, and beginning the process of adapting these practices to his or her own values and belief system. When finished, it may be useful to have clients include this material in work they do with recovery program sponsors on any of the steps that discuss God or a Higher Power.

# UNDERSTANDING SPIRITUALITY
# IN 12-STEP PROGRAMS

This assignment is designed to help you begin working through an issue that troubles many people new to recovery programs. This is a big subject, and one handout cannot cover it all, but it can offer some pointers to get started.

Why work on spirituality? Because it can make the difference between living clean and sober or dying drunk or addicted. It is the most important key to effective use of Alcoholics Anonymous (AA), Narcotics Anonymous (NA), and other 12-step programs.

When people attend their first meetings of 12-step programs and find they don't like the meetings, the most common reason is that they are uncomfortable with talk about God. This may appear to be a barrier making these programs useless to them, but it doesn't have to be.

Many people have good reasons to feel skeptical about religion. They may have had bad experiences with religious people or institutions. Perhaps they just feel that God has not been there in their lives.

Maybe they belong to a non-Christian faith that doesn't use the name God or the term *Higher Power*. Hearing God or a Higher Power mentioned in 7 of the 12 steps may be an immediate turnoff.

Or perhaps the idea that God is male offends some people, and the references to God as Him, He, and so on offends them. For some, the practice in many groups of ending meetings with the Lord's Prayer, which refers to God as Our Father, can also be offensive, particularly if their biological fathers were abusive or neglectful and father is not a word they feel good about. For this reason, some 12-step programs or groups use gender-neutral language in the steps. However, you are likely to find yourself in meetings where the readings refer to God as He and Him.

Finally, the individual expressions by members of a group of their relationships with the Higher Power of their understanding may include references to specific religious beliefs and practices that are different from yours, and this may take some getting used to.

However, many people who did not believe in God or believed that no one could know whether God exists have found that they can use AA, NA, and other 12-step programs to make the changes they want to make in their lives. You can learn to overlook the words and phrases drawn from conventional Christianity, the religion of most of the people who wrote the AA Big Book, and draw meanings you can use to help you achieve the recovery you want but haven't been able to accomplish with your best efforts. *The point is to understand the difference between spirituality and religion.*

1. Write down your description of religion. What do you think of when you hear the word?

   _____

   _____

   _____

   _____

2. Now think about the word spirituality and write your definition for this word:

   _____

   _____

   _____

   _____

3. Are there differences in the meanings of religion and spirituality for you? _____ If so, what is the biggest difference you see?

   _____

   _____

   _____

   _____

A definition of religion could go like this:

> A religion is a specific system of practices and rituals, based on a belief in a specific divine or superhuman power, usually practiced through membership in a specific human organization, usually called a church.

A similar definition for spirituality might sound like this:

> Spirituality is a focus on the moral aspects of life, on doing what is right, and will help us become the best people we are capable of being.

You could say it this way: A religion is a system created by people to achieve spirituality. You could think of spirituality as water and religion as a bottle, a container to hold water. But other containers can hold water, and some bottles contain other things instead of water.

4. Does this idea make sense to you? _____ What other containers for spirituality can you think of that help you focus on what is right in life?

_____

_____

_____

_____

_____

5. At this point, you may be thinking, "Doesn't this definition of religion also describe a 12-step program? It seems to be a specific system of practices and rituals, and it is practiced through membership in a specific organization!" Have you had the thought that AA, NA, or some other 12-step program seemed to resemble a church? If so, what similarities do you see?

_____

_____

_____

_____

_____

6. What differences do you see between 12-step groups and churches?

_____

_____

_____

_____

7. Here are three key differences between 12-step groups and churches:

   1. <u>Specific definitions of God</u>: A church or religion offers specific ways to understand God, and may insist that no other way is correct. A 12-step program asks you to think in terms of a power greater than yourself and leaves it to you to decide what that power is and how it works.

      As evidence of this, listen for people expressing different understandings of a Higher Power. Depending on whether their beliefs are Catholic; Orthodox; Jewish; Muslim; Protestant; Hindu; Buddhist; any of many Native American faith systems; or just a personal, noninstitutional faith in a Higher Power that is not quite like anyone else's; in a healthy group you will see acceptance of whatever works for each individual.

   2. <u>Authority</u>: While a church normally has a formal hierarchy and structure of people in charge, in a 12-step group no one is in charge; there is no chain of command. Decisions are made by the group through a vote called a *group conscience.* No one can give orders; and if anyone tries, they are usually set straight quickly by the other members of the group.

   3. <u>Membership requirements</u>: Religions may restrict their memberships in many ways: by birth, heritage, or obedience to various rules. By contrast, in any 12-step program, Tradition 3 says that the only membership requirement is a desire to solve the problem that the group exists to overcome. Anyone who wants to be a member can do so, and no one can be excluded. You don't have to be clean and sober, merely trying to get that way. Certain groups may have restrictions. There are nonsmoking

groups, groups for men or women, and so on, but a 12-step program as a whole is open to anyone who wants to participate.

How might these differences make a 12-step program work differently from a church?

_____

_____

_____

_____

8. Going back to the definition of spirituality, how do you think that paying attention to the moral aspects of life and what is right could help you solve the problems facing you with alcohol, other drugs, or other addictive behaviors?

_____

_____

_____

_____

If you see that a focus on these parts of your life could be useful, that's all it takes to include spirituality in your recovery work. If you don't have a belief in a Higher Power that can help you stay clean and sober, Steps 2 and 3 and the help of others in recovery can guide you in figuring out what works best for you.

Be sure to bring this handout to your next session with your therapist and talk about your thoughts and feelings about the exercise.

# FINDING A HOME GROUP

## GOALS OF THIS EXERCISE

1. Learn about reasons and methods for finding and working with a 12-step home group.

2. Strengthen interpersonal support networks and reduce social isolation.

3. Enhance 12-step work and reduce the likelihood of relapse into addiction or addictive behaviors.

4. Accelerate learning improved social and communication skills by frequent interaction with others in a healthy community setting.

## SUGGESTIONS FOR PROCESSING THIS EXERCISE WITH CLIENTS

This exercise is designed for newly recovering clients who are having difficulty affiliating with recovery programs or are drawn to negative peer influences. It provides an explanation of the purpose and workings of home groups and guides clients in selecting a group and forming a connection. This applies to groups organized around many issues. Follow-up for this exercise could include journaling about the experience and reporting back to the therapist, treatment group, and program sponsor and encouraging the client to become more involved in the home group through service work and participation in social activities.

# FINDING A HOME GROUP

One of the things often mentioned in 12-step meetings is having a home group, and many groups routinely invite newcomers to adopt those meetings as their home groups. This worksheet will help you choose a home group and get the most out of participating in that group. It is a good idea to talk over everything on this sheet, as well as any other questions or ideas you have, with your therapist.

What is a home group for? Let's look at why people call a group a *home group.*

1. When you hear the word *home* what thoughts come to your mind?

    _____

    _____

    _____

    _____

2. To different people, home can mean any or all of these things:

    • A place where they are known and accepted.

    • A place where they are safe and can relax.

    • A place where they are loved.

    • A place where they are missed if they aren't there.

    • A place where they share important parts of their lives with others who care about them.

    • A place where they are involved in important decisions that affect them and others.

For many people, though, the word *home* brings up different thoughts. Their homes may not have been safe or loving. If that's true for you, maybe you wish your home had fit the description above, but it didn't. A good home group could become the home you never got as a child.

Either way, how many of these qualities are important to you? Please circle the qualities in question 2 that you want to find. What are other situations where you've found these things in your life?

_____

_____

_____

3. Some places many people have found those things include: churches, social clubs, gangs, athletic teams, the military, or their jobs. Have any of these situations given you the things connected with the word *home* above? If so, which ones?

_____

_____

_____

4. Now think about people you see socializing before, during, or after 12-step meetings. Did they seem to be finding some or all of the things we just listed in those meetings? Which things?

_____

_____

_____

5. As we said previously, some people grew up in families where addiction or other problems caused serious problems and they didn't feel good about home. People in this situation can feel lonely, as if they don't fit in anywhere, and may look for replacement families to fill the needs their childhood families couldn't. They often try to soothe these feelings with alcohol or other drugs. How often do you feel this way? Are there places, groups, or activities you have used to escape this kind of loneliness? If so, how has it worked?

_____

_____

_____

6. A home group is a group you choose to formally join and attend regularly. You may find your sponsor there or take on responsibilities, such as making coffee, cleaning up, or being the treasurer. You will probably participate in the group's business meeting, referred to as a group conscience.

Many people think of their home groups as their second families—families they have chosen—that meet their needs for family ties in ways their birth families may not be able to do. How would you feel about the idea of belonging to a second family like this?

_____

_____

_____

_____

7. In attending different meetings, you may have noticed that you feel most comfortable in certain types of groups. What meetings or kind of meetings make you feel most at home?

_____

_____

_____

_____

8. In the meetings you like, have you noticed people treating each other with caring and respect and enjoying each other's company?

_____

_____

_____

_____

9. How could belonging to such a group help you cope with and solve problems in your life?

_____

_____

_____

_____

10. What could you do to contribute to such a group?

_____

_____

_____

_____

11. Whether or not your treatment program requires you to choose a home group, it will help your recovery to do so. Please name a group that you feel might be good as your home group:

_____

_____

_____

_____

12. What is it about that group that appeals to you more than other groups?

_____

_____

_____

_____

13. When and where does this group meet, and how often will you attend?

_____

_____

_____

_____

Be sure to bring this handout to your next session with your therapist and talk about your thoughts and feelings about the exercise.

# LEARNING FROM RECOVERY ROLE MODELS

## GOALS OF THIS EXERCISE

1. Learn from others who are succeeding in solving the same problems.

2. Form a healthy bond with a community of like-minded people pursuing the same goals.

3. Increase healthy interdependence with others rather than either enmeshed codependence or unsupported isolation.

## SUGGESTIONS FOR PROCESSING THIS EXERCISE WITH CLIENTS

This exercise is designed for newly recovering clients who may be either hesitant about forming relationships with fellow recovering people or vulnerable to being negatively influenced by others whose example will not help them to achieve and maintain recovery. Its approach is to guide clients in choosing appropriate role models and then provide a structured way to approach them and form supportive connections. Follow-up might include assignments to continue researching and experimenting with methods used by clients who succeed in recovery, journaling about these experiences, and applying the information gathered. When finished, the information collected in this exercise may be useful in completing personal recovery or relapse prevention plans.

# LEARNING FROM RECOVERY ROLE MODELS

Most recovering addicts say one of the best experiences they have when they get involved in recovery work, either through therapy or a support group, is that for the first time they feel that they fit in—they have found people who are like them. It makes sense that what works for these other people, who have gone through the same experiences as the newly recovering person, might work for the newly recovering person as well. In this exercise you will learn about what has worked for others who have a lot in common with you, methods that might help you as well.

1. Since starting treatment, have you met people who are like you and who are successfully staying clean and sober? If you have tried to quit before without success, does it give you more hope to see others like you succeed? How have your thoughts about recovery changed?

   _____

   _____

   _____

   _____

2. When you talk with someone like you who is succeeding at changing addictive patterns you are trying to overcome, what do they tell you are the most important things they do to succeed?

   _____

   _____

   _____

   _____

3. Here are some things that people do to stay clean and sober. Please check the ones you see or hear others using:

____ Avoid places they practiced addictions.

____ Talk to supportive people when stressed.

____ Avoid people they practiced with.

____ Go to therapy.

____ Go to support group meetings (AA, etc.).

____ Work with a 12-step sponsor.

____ Be a 12-step sponsor for others.

____ Socialize with sober friends.

____ Laugh at least once a day.

____ Make a recovery/relapse prevention plan.

____ Go to church.

____ Get regular exercise.

____ Read recovery/spiritual material.

____ Keep a journal.

____ Help others stay clean and sober.

____ Pray daily.

____ HALT: Don't get too **H**ungry, **A**ngry, **L**onely, or **T**ired.

4. During the next week, your homework assignment is to talk to a different recovering person each day and ask what actions he or she takes to help stay clean and sober. Write their answers here:

Day 1:

_____

_____

_____

Day 2:

_____

_____

_____

Day 3:

_____

_____

_____

Day 4:

_____

_____

_____

Day 5:

_____

_____

_____

Day 6:

_____

_____

_____

Day 7:

_____

_____

_____

5. Now choose the methods best suited to your personality and your situation. Ideally, everyone should have four types of strategies to stay sober. You want strategies that you can use alone and strategies allowing you and others to help one another. You will also want strategies for very specific situations and strategies that are

useful for nearly all situations. Please fill in this grid with at least two methods per square:

|  | Methods to Use Alone | Methods to Use with Others |
|---|---|---|
| Methods for specific situations that would challenge you (e.g., a high-stress situation or an invitation to go drinking with your best friend) |  |  |
| Methods for general use in any situation |  |  |

6. Finally, it's useful to notice what has *not* worked for others, especially others like you. Your assignment is to talk to at least five recovering people or bring up this topic in a therapy or support group meeting and ask them what they have seen others try or have tried themselves to avoid relapse, but without succeeding. List some actions that didn't work for those who tried them:

_____

_____

_____

_____

Be sure to bring this handout to your next session with your therapist and talk about your thoughts and feelings about the exercise.

# FINDING AND WORKING WITH A 12-STEP SPONSOR

## GOALS OF THIS EXERCISE

1. Learn about reasons and methods for finding and working with a 12-step program sponsor.

2. Strengthen interpersonal support networks and reduce social isolation.

3. Enhance 12-step work and reduce the likelihood of relapse into addiction or addictive behaviors.

4. Accelerate learning improved thinking and coping skills by exposure to those used by others with success on similar issues.

## SUGGESTIONS FOR PROCESSING THIS EXERCISE WITH CLIENTS

This exercise is designed for newly recovering clients who are reluctant to affiliate and get actively involved with recovery work in a 12-step program or are drawn to negative peer influences. It provides an explanation of the purpose and workings of the sponsor relationship and guides clients in selecting a prospective sponsor, approaching that person, and structuring interaction afterward. This applies to groups organized around many issues. Follow-up for this exercise could include journaling about the experience and reporting back to the therapist, treatment group, and program sponsor.

# FINDING AND WORKING WITH A 12-STEP SPONSOR

One of the first things most people hear at 12-step meetings is much talk about sponsors and frequent advice on finding one. This worksheet will help you in that process.

1. Why do I need a sponsor? To start out, please describe your general impression of what a sponsor is and what he or she would do for you:

   _____

   _____

   _____

   _____

   _____

2. Some other words that people use to describe a sponsor might include these: teacher, coach, tutor, mentor, or guide. Do these words give you a different mental picture than the first one you had when you heard people talking about sponsors? If so, how are the two pictures different?

   _____

   _____

   _____

   _____

   _____

3. Have you learned skills in the past with the help of a teacher, coach, or tutor? How were these people able to help you?

   _____

   _____

   _____

   _____

4. If you're like most people, you find that the qualities that make others most helpful to you in learning new skills include the following:

   • They are respectful to you.

   • They understand you.

   • They use terms you can understand.

   • They know what they're talking about.

   • They are encouraging.

   • They find a balance between pushing you and being patient with you.

   Now think of the people you've learned from in the past who were the biggest help to you. Which of the qualities we just listed did they have?

   _____

   _____

   _____

   _____

5. How would it be to have someone like that help you with your questions and problems in getting clean and sober?

   _____

   _____

   _____

   _____

6. How could you find a person like this to work with you?

_____

_____

_____

_____

7. Do you have a problem with the idea of someone helping you learn skills for achieving clean and sober life? If so, what bothers you about this idea?

_____

_____

_____

_____

8. How can you overcome these objections so that you are able to work with a sponsor? What could a possible sponsor, your therapist, or your group do to help you with this?

_____

_____

_____

_____

9. Here are some recommendations offered by people experienced in working with a sponsor. They will often say that a sponsor should have the following characteristics:

- Someone who says things in meetings that you find help you with your own questions

- Someone you feel comfortable with and feel you could trust

- Someone who has his or her own sponsor and works with that sponsor regularly

- Someone who has worked the 12 steps himself or herself and has at least a year of clean and sober time

- Someone who seems to have a balanced life without crises

- Someone with whom there is no possibility of developing a sexual attraction to interfere with your recovery work

- Someone who is not already in a close family, work, or friendship relationship with you

During the next few meetings you attend, pick out some people who seem to fit this profile and list their names here:

_____

_____

_____

_____

10. Of the people you have listed, who would be most helpful to you in learning to work a 12-step program and handle life's issues without relapsing?

_____

_____

_____

_____

11. How will you approach this person and ask him or her to be your sponsor?

_____

_____

_____

_____

12. When will you do this? Pick a time, talk it over with your therapist, and follow through.

_____

_____

_____

_____

13. To be answered after you find a sponsor: What was it like asking this person to be your sponsor? How did you feel, and what did you expect to happen?

_____

_____

_____

_____

14. When and where will you talk with your sponsor each week?

_____

_____

_____

_____

Be sure to bring this handout to your next session with your therapist and talk about your thoughts and feelings about the exercise.

# 12-STEP MEETING REVIEW/ CRITIQUE FORM

## GOALS OF THIS EXERCISE

1. Assess the client's participation and areas of attention in attending 12-step meetings.

2. Prompt the client to identify similarities between his/her experiences and those of others at meetings.

3. Identify areas of confusion or resistance related to 12-step meetings for therapeutic attention.

4. Suggest types/formats of meetings most likely to be accepted by the client.

## SUGGESTIONS FOR PROCESSING THIS EXERCISE WITH CLIENTS

This exercise is designed to help clinicians assess clients' participation in 12-step meetings and prompt clients to greater attention and consideration of the content of meetings. In addition, it will help ensure that clients actually attend meetings rather than falsifying signature sheets. It would be more difficult to convincingly fabricate answers to questions or discuss those answers with a therapist if the client had not actually gone to the meeting. Here are some useful questions for discussion with the client when following up on meeting attendance:

1. What other kinds of meetings have you attended?

2. What kind of meeting do you think would be the best fit for you?

3. Were there people that seemed more different from you than they turned out to be when they talked about their lives?

4. If you had talked about your experiences related to this topic, what might you have said?

In addition, if more than one client in a group attend the same meeting, their responses to this exercise may form a useful basis for group discussion.

# 12-STEP MEETING REVIEW/ CRITIQUE FORM

Do not take this form to a meeting with you, and do not write down people's names or other information that would violate anyone's anonymity or confidentiality or violate a 12-step program's traditions in any other way. Instead, fill it out soon after the meeting while the details are fresh in your memory.

1. Meeting information:

    Program (AA, NA, etc.): _____

    Location: _____

    Date/time: _____

    Meeting format: (   ) Tag/open sharing

                          (   ) Speaking meeting

                          (   ) Book study

                          (   ) Step study

                          (   ) All male/all female

                          (   ) Young people's

                          (   ) Other: _____

2. What was the main topic of the meeting?

    _____

    _____

    _____

    _____

    _____

3. What were your general thoughts and feelings on that topic?

_____

_____

_____

_____

4. In what ways could you relate to the experiences and feelings shared by others at the meeting? Were you unable to relate to some people, and if so, what was the difference between them and you that made it hard to relate?

_____

_____

_____

_____

5. What other thoughts and feelings did this meeting cause you to have?

_____

_____

_____

_____

6. What did you gain from this meeting?

_____

_____

_____

_____

Be sure to bring this handout to your next session with your therapist and talk about your thoughts and feelings about the exercise.

# STEP 1: UNDERSTANDING POWERLESSNESS

## GOALS OF THIS EXERCISE

1. Identify instances when substance use or other addictive behavior has gotten out of control.

2. Learn that others have overcome similar problems.

3. Begin working the 12 steps.

## SUGGESTIONS FOR PROCESSING THIS EXERCISE WITH CLIENTS

This exercise is designed for clients who are at or near hitting bottom and are either motivated for change or ambivalent. It works to normalize the experience of powerlessness to reduce the client's sense of isolation, while increasing motivation to begin recovery work and providing a better understanding of Step 1, the entry point to any 12-step recovery program. Follow-up could include the exercises devoted to the remaining steps, finding and working with a 12-step sponsor, and finding a home group, as well as sharing the outcome of these activities with the therapist, treatment group, and a program sponsor.

# STEP 1: UNDERSTANDING POWERLESSNESS

This assignment is designed to help you work the first step in your 12-step program. If you have already worked Step 1, please use this hand-out to record the answers you found to these questions when you worked that step.

What does powerlessness mean? Most people have a difficult time accepting that they can't control things they thought they could, especially if other people are not powerless in these areas. Many people are powerless over alcohol and other drugs; other people and their actions; compulsive behaviors such as gambling, spending money, or overeating; and sometimes even their own feelings.

The idea that they might be powerless is both unpleasant and hard to believe for many people. However, if they really are powerless, denying it does not improve their lives. It just leaves them off guard and less able to avoid danger or pain. Step 1 helps people see themselves and the world around them realistically and to stop stumbling into pitfalls because they don't see them under their feet.

You don't have to be out of control all the time to be powerless. Losing control once in a while may be all it takes to make your life unmanageable.

Many people trying to understand what has happened because of their addictive behavior start out with ideas of what powerlessness means that don't fit them and convince themselves they aren't powerless. Look over these statements and check any you have said or thought:

\_\_\_ If I was powerless, I'd be drinking or using all the time. I only drink (on weekends, at night, at home, out of town, etc.), so I'm not powerless!

___ If I was powerless, I'd be unable to stop once I started every time I drank/used/did that. Some/most of the time, I can stop when I want to, so I'm not powerless!

___ If I was powerless, I'd be (homeless, unable to hold a job/care for my kids/pay my bills, etc.). I function pretty well and do what's expected of me, so I'm not powerless!

___ If I was powerless, I'd be getting arrested, getting DUIs, and so on. I've never been in trouble connected with this, so I'm not powerless!

It may help to consider it this way. Suppose you were shopping for a car, and a salesperson showed you a nice-looking car and said this to you:

> This one's a lot of fun, and the steering wheel and the brakes work most of the time. Once in a while it won't go where you try to steer it, and every now and then it doesn't stop when you try to hit the brakes—but that only happens occasionally, and no car is perfect.

Would you buy that car?

If a driver is powerless over his or her car one time in a hundred, most drivers would feel that was enough powerlessness to be a serious problem.

If a person is powerless over what happens when he or she drinks or uses or takes some other action one time in a hundred, that is enough powerlessness to be a serious problem. If the consequences are dangerous (physically, financially, or emotionally) to important relationships, it is as dangerous as that car we just thought about.

1. Please read through the following and check any items that are true in your life:

   ___ I have done something while (drinking/using/engaging in this behavior) that I didn't mean to do or that I definitely intended not to do.

   ___ I have found myself (drinking/using/engaging in this behavior) when I didn't plan to and had said I wouldn't.

   ___ I have found myself (drinking/using/engaging in this behavior) more or for longer than I planned when I started.

____ I have quit, or tried to quit (drinking/using/engaging in this behavior) and found that I could not quit or could not stay quit, even though I really wanted to and really tried.

____ I have suffered humiliation, serious problems, or physical or emotional pain on more than one occasion because of my (drinking/using/engaging in this behavior), but I have continued to do it.

____ When I have gone for more than a day or two without (drinking/using/engaging in this behavior), I have felt physically sick (shaking, sweating, feeling too hot or too cold, muscle spasms, nausea) or have felt emotionally sick (craving for the substance or activity, anxiety or panic, depression, being easy to anger, sometimes even seeing, hearing, or feeling things that weren't there) and found that I got immediate relief when I (drank/used/engaged in the behavior).

2. Describe two times when you lost control of how much you did or how much time or money you spent on alcohol, another drug, or a problem behavior.

_____

_____

_____

_____

_____

3. Give examples of things you have done because of these losses of control that were bad for your health, career, relationships, or other important parts of your life.

_____

_____

_____

_____

_____

4. Give examples of ways you have tried to control this situation in your life.

_____

_____

_____

5. How do you feel about the idea that you are powerless in this matter?

_____

_____

_____

6. Many feel it's not okay to be powerless. No one likes it! Alcoholics and addicts in particular tend to be their own harshest judges. Give examples of negative judgments you have made of yourself because of your inability to control the substance or behavior in your life.

_____

_____

_____

7. Part of addiction is that people's unwillingness to face this power-lessness and their harsh judgment of themselves make them dis-honest with themselves and with others. They lie about their actions, motives, thoughts, and feelings because it would be too uncomfortable to admit the truth. This dishonesty spreads to other parts of their lives. Give some examples of dishonesty in your life:

_____

_____

_____

8. How has the deceptive behavior you described worked in your life? What were the results?

_____

_____

_____

9. What would happen if you were honest with yourself and others about these things?

_____

_____

_____

10. Think of other people you know who have done similar things. How were you affected by their dishonesty?

_____

_____

_____

11. The other side of powerlessness is lack of responsibility. If you have no power over a thing, you can't be responsible for it. When you deny your powerlessness, you feel responsible for things you don't control. What are some things you feel responsible for that you don't have any control over?

_____

_____

_____

12. How has feeling responsible for these things affected your life?

_____

_____

_____

13. What would happen if you stopped trying to control things you can't control?

_____

_____

_____

14. Many people feel that saying they are powerless would mean that they had no responsibility for *anything,* and that this would be a cop-out. Are there things you really are responsible for that you have blamed on other people or things outside yourself? If so, what are some of them?

_____

_____

_____

15. How has holding others responsible for your actions affected your life?

_____

_____

_____

16. How would your life be affected if you accepted responsibility for these things?

_____

_____

_____

17. Think of someone for whom you have great respect. What are some things that person is powerless over, and how has he or she handled that powerlessness?

_____

_____

_____

18. Often, when people see someone accept things he or she can't control with calm and serenity, it increases their respect for that person. Does the powerlessness of the person you respect in the areas you just mentioned reduce the respect you and others have felt for them?

_____

_____

_____

The second part of Step 1 says that "our lives had become unmanageable." What does the word *unmanageable* mean to you?

_____

_____

_____

Now do an exercise in imagination: Picture yourself in the future, living a life in which you are honest with yourself and others about what you have power over, what you're powerless over, and what is manageable and unmanageable in your life. How would others feel about you? How would you feel about yourself? Please write a short description of how you think this life would be different from your life now and talk about this with your therapist and your sponsor.

_____

_____

_____

_____

_____

_____

Be sure to bring this handout to your next session with your therapist and talk about your thoughts and feelings about the exercise.

# STEP 2: FINDING HOPE

## GOALS OF THIS EXERCISE

1. Continue to work the 12 steps.

2. Identify spiritual issues for therapeutic work.

3. Increase awareness of ways 12-step programs can be adapted to fit the client's value system.

## SUGGESTIONS FOR PROCESSING THIS EXERCISE WITH CLIENTS

This exercise is designed for clients who have begun working the 12 steps in Alcoholics Anonymous or another 12-step program and have completed Step 1. Its purpose is to provide hope and motivation by changing clients' mind-set of isolated self-sufficiency. Follow-up would include the exercises devoted to the remaining steps and the assignment titled "Understanding Spirituality in 12-Step Programs," as well as sharing the outcome of this activity with the therapist, treatment group, and program sponsor.

# STEP 2: FINDING HOPE

This assignment is designed to help you work Step 2. If you have already worked Step 2 with your sponsor, please use this handout to record the work you did then.

Do you need to be restored to sanity? If you're like most people, it was difficult enough to accept that you were powerless in Step 1. Now this next step is calling you crazy, too! Think about it—how could anything *restore* you to sanity unless you had lost your sanity to start with? And yet this can be a great source of hope.

With Step 1 and the realization that you are powerless over things that could kill you or ruin your life, you face a terrible situation. Most addicts and alcoholics already knew inside that they were out of control—"that our lives had become unmanageable"—and that may have caused them a lot of depression and anxiety. If they had to stay stuck at that point, the future would be very dark.

However, Step 2 says that being powerless doesn't mean your life has to *stay* out of control. You may find happiness and peace through "a power greater than ourselves." That's why many people call this the "hope step."

1. Do you feel your life has been insane? _____ What does *sanity* mean to you?

   _____

   _____

   _____

2. What do you think of the idea of a Higher Power?

   _____

   _____

   _____

3. What experiences have you had that have led you to this view of a Higher Power?

_____

_____

_____

_____

4. How have you tried to make your life more sane than it was? How well did your efforts work?

_____

_____

_____

_____

5. If your life has been out of control, and you've tried to straighten it out but couldn't, can you believe that a power greater than you could do this? _____ Would you want this to happen?

_____

_____

_____

_____

6. Here are some alternatives to the idea that a Higher Power could restore us to sanity. If one of these fits your beliefs better, please circle that letter.

   a. My life is not insane at all; I am in control and things are the way I want them to be.

   b. My life is insane but I can straighten things out myself.

   c. My life is insane but there is nothing either I or any Higher Power can do about it.

7. What would you have to gain and to lose if it were true that there was a Higher Power that could create the order in your life that you may have wanted but been unable to produce?

What I would have to gain: _____

_____

_____

_____

What I would have to lose: _____

_____

_____

_____

8. If you are unable to believe in the idea of a Higher Power that can make your life better, do you wish you could believe it? How would it change things if there were such a Higher Power?

_____

_____

_____

_____

9. Think of your sponsor or other people from your 12-step program that you like and respect. Have you talked about the Higher Power with these people? What were their views?

_____

_____

_____

_____

10. Have you heard a different explanation of God or a Higher Power that made sense to you? In general, what was it?

_____

_____

_____

_____

11. Think about a Higher Power or God that would be good and would make sense to you but would fit this world where bad things happen to good people. If you can imagine such a Higher Power or God, what would that Power be like?

_____

_____

_____

_____

12. If you have trouble believing in God, would it make a difference if you experienced an event or a feeling of having a Higher Power present? If you imagined a good version of a Higher Power that would make sense to you, how would that Power affect people's lives?

_____

_____

_____

_____

13. If such a Higher Power existed, how would you personally be able to tell? How would you see evidence of that Power's actions? Would there be things to notice? What would they be?

_____

_____

_____

_____

14. How would your life be affected if there was a Higher Power doing the kinds of things in your life that the 12-step programs describe?

_____

_____

_____

_____

15. What would have to happen or what would you have to see for you to believe there was a Higher Power trying to help you?

_____

_____

_____

_____

16. Look back over your life and think about whether you have had experiences where a Higher Power may have been helping you. What happened, and how have you explained it to yourself?

_____

_____

_____

_____

17. If you find yourself unable to definitely believe in the idea of a Higher Power, can you think of it as an unanswered question, with an open mind? What does it feel like to admit that it is at least possible? Does this cause you to feel any hope, or fear, or both?

_____

_____

_____

_____

Be sure to bring this handout to your next session with your therapist and talk about your thoughts and feelings about the exercise.

# STEP 3: DECIDING TO TURN IT OVER

## GOALS OF THIS EXERCISE

1. Continue to work the 12 Steps.

2. Think about the idea of turning one's will and life over to the care of a Higher Power.

3. Increase understanding of how people resolve spiritual issues in 12-step programs.

## SUGGESTIONS FOR PROCESSING THIS EXERCISE WITH CLIENTS

This exercise is designed to help clients through the first step requiring a commitment to change. It guides them in analyzing the words of the step phrase by phrase, then in contemplating what a positive relationship with a Higher Power might be like, using other nurturing relationships as metaphors and determining what the benefits might be. Follow-up would include the exercises devoted to the remaining steps, as well as sharing the work done in this activity and its outcome with the therapist, treatment group, and program sponsor.

# STEP 3: DECIDING TO TURN IT OVER

This assignment is designed to help you work Step 3. Whether or not you have worked this step before, it is a good idea to go through this handout with your 12-step sponsor and your therapist.

Step 1 asks people to admit some things that they may not have been able to see clearly at first. One of those things was that they were powerless over a substance or behavior, and the other was that their lives were out of control. Step 2 asked them to accept that it was possible that some power greater than themselves could straighten out the craziness.

Neither of the first two steps calls for any action—they are thinking steps. Now Step 3 asks you to make a decision to turn your will and your life over to the care of God.

Most people don't like this idea. First of all, people in this society have usually been raised to believe they should be in control of their own lives. The idea of turning over control to anyone or anything else sounds crazy, like letting go of the steering wheel in traffic. Second, many have had bad experiences with religion, or they may have cried out to God in despair and pain and seen nothing change.

The 12-step experiences of millions of people since 1935 seem to show that a relationship with a Higher Power may be helpful. Many of those people are highly intelligent and not likely to be conned or brainwashed; many started out with the same doubts and suspicions about God that you may have now. But for millions of people like you, this step came to make sense, and the results show that it seems to work.

1. Are you comfortable with what this step asks you to do? _____
   If you aren't, what part bothers you, or what do you feel you might
   have a hard time doing?

   _____

   _____

   _____

2. You've probably done your best to solve your own problems before
   this. You've given them your best thought and your hardest efforts,
   but your best often hasn't worked. What benefits do you think you
   might see if there was a God or Higher Power greater than yourself
   that would help you, and you were able to turn your problems over
   to this God or Higher Power?

   _____

   _____

   _____

3. Some people recommend breaking this step down into phrases and
   examining them one by one. The first phrase is "Made a decision."
   What does "making a decision" mean to you?

   _____

   _____

   _____

4. "Made a decision" sounds like a shift from thinking to acting—the
   action can be right now or in the future. Are you ready to decide on
   strong action to change your life? If you still need to think about it
   for a while you can do that. The step doesn't say that once you
   make this decision you have to "turn your will and your life over"
   today. It says you *decide* you will do so. Does thinking of it this
   way change the way this step sounds to you? If so, how?

   _____

   _____

   _____

5. Are you ready to decide you will act, even if not today? If you're stuck at this point, talk with your sponsor or a friend who's already gone through this. Find out how they felt and what happened. Other than talking with a friend or your sponsor, what can you do to find out more about this step and to get answers for any questions or difficulties you have with it?

_____

_____

_____

_____

6. The next phrase is "to turn our will and our lives over." Have you had painful experiences with entrusting others with things that were important to you, such as possessions, information, decisions, or even your safety or the safety of someone else, and had them let you down? _____ Do you feel this has happened with God or a Higher Power? _____ If you answered "Yes" to either of these, what happened and how did you feel about it?

_____

_____

_____

_____

7. A big part of trust is learning *how much* trust you can give a person or thing. If you trust them to do something they can't or won't do, you'll be disappointed and possibly hurt. Has someone failed to do what you trusted them to do? Can you see now that they didn't have the ability or character to do it? What happened, and how do you feel about it now?

_____

_____

_____

_____

8. To go on thinking about that last question and avoid feeling let down by God, you need to have a realistic understanding of what God can and will do. That brings us to the last phrase in this step: "to the care of God *as we understood God.*" Those last four words are very important.

   This step doesn't ask you to trust someone else's version of God or a Higher Power. It asks you to set aside whatever you've been taught about God and start over. It requires you to figure out for yourself what kind of God or Higher Power makes sense to you. How can you figure out for yourself what God or a Higher Power might really be like?

   _____

   _____

   _____

9. Here is one way that has worked for other people.
   a. Find a quiet place to sit and think. God is often referred to as a father. This may make you uneasy if your father was someone you couldn't trust and feel safe with. But think about being a parent. If you have children, think about how you feel about them, and if you don't have kids, think about how you would want to treat them if you did. First think about what you can do for your children. List some things you can do for them:

   _____

   _____

   _____

   b. Now think about the limits of what you can do for your children. What are the things you'd like to do for them, but can't? List some of the dangers you can't protect them from:

   _____

   _____

   _____

10. Can you protect your children from all the results of their own actions?

    As a parent you can do your best to teach your children, to advise and warn them, but sometimes they still do things you know will hurt them and others. Often they may hurt you. How does it feel to think about your children making mistakes and being hurt or hurting someone else in spite of your efforts to teach and warn them?

    _____

    _____

    _____

    _____

11. Some recovering people believe in a God who really is like a parent, who gives God's children much of what they need and can teach and advise them, but who can't make them listen or take away their free will. Because this God will not take away their free will, God can't keep these children from doing things that hurt them or others. This God gives support and guidance as well as comfort and healing after bad things happen but can't prevent many bad things that do happen. How does this compare with your picture of yourself as a parent?

    _____

    _____

    _____

    _____

12. Now think about the experiences you have had in your life and the world as you see it around you. Would a God like this make sense in this world and still be able to help you with your recovery from being dependent on a drug? If such a God existed, how could you tell?

    _____

    _____

    _____

    _____

13. One way many people feel they could tell God was there would be that God would help them when they needed help. Think back on your life. Were there times when something happened at just the right time for you in a way that seems hard to believe? Times when your luck was better than anyone would expect? What happened?

_____

_____

_____

_____

14. Another piece of evidence to look for is the advice a good parent gives his or her children. To see whether God has given us advice and warnings, we would need to know how God might communicate with us. Many people say that there were times when they felt a kind of inner voice—a hunch, gut feeling, intuition, conscience—urging them not to do something and giving them an uneasy feeling about it. What experiences have you had like that?

_____

_____

_____

_____

15. When you ignored that inner voice or feeling, what were the results?

_____

_____

_____

_____

16. Do you think that inner voice could have been a way for your God to give you advice? If that makes sense, how do you feel about the idea that God has been talking to you from within?

_____

_____

_____

_____

17. Another way some people feel God reaches out to them is through other people. What experiences have you had of someone showing up at just the right time in your life and helping you or telling you something you needed to hear?

_____

_____

_____

18. Do you think that could have been another way for God to communicate with you, and if so, how do you feel about that idea?

_____

_____

_____

19. If this way of thinking about God makes sense for you, it still leaves the question of how to "turn our will and our lives over." Since this idea of God is about a being who helps people mainly by providing help and guidance, what would "turning it over" mean, so that you wouldn't be hurt by expecting God to do things God wouldn't do?

_____

_____

_____

20. For many people who find this way of thinking about God useful, "turning it over" means looking to God for emotional support and guidance. Do you feel you could listen for the guidance of your inner voice or conscience and follow that guidance? How would your life be different up to now if you based your choices and actions on that guidance rather than on your impulses, fears, desires, and compulsions?

_____

_____

_____

21. If you feel this makes sense, it's one way to do Step 3. You can seek God's guidance and support from your inner voice and then trust and follow that guidance and watch for the support of God in the good other people bring to you in your daily life.

    There's another side. Since you also play a role in other people's lives, this would also mean that God has acted through you. Have you ever been the one who was there at just the right time for someone else? What happened? How did you help them?

    _____

    _____

    _____

    _____

    _____

22. How does it feel to think that you might be evidence of God in the life of someone else?

    _____

    _____

    _____

    _____

    _____

23. If this discussion of God as a parent has not helped, there are other ways to think about the nature of God. Some people think of God in ways guided by Native American beliefs. Others think of something like the "Force." These are the important things to do:

    a. Spend time thinking about it and decide for yourself what kind of God could exist, based on the experiences and information you have, and could be helpful to you.

    b. Decide how you could tell whether God did exist. What evidence would there be?

    c. Look for evidence and events that are hard to explain any other way.

24. Would you want the benefits of a good relationship with a God you could trust to help you? _____ If you would, what would you be willing to do to have that in your life?

    _____

    _____

    _____

25. Now do another imagination exercise. Imagine a future in which you have found answers to your questions and troubled feelings about God. Imagine knowing you could count on the guidance and support of a Higher Power. See yourself living with confidence and peace of mind and knowing that you will never face a problem alone again. How does it make you feel?

    _____

    _____

    _____

26. What can you do to start moving toward that life?

    _____

    _____

    _____

If you still aren't ready for Step 3, go back and spend more time on Steps 1 and 2. If you aren't ready to turn your will and life over yet, don't give up on AA, NA, or another 12-step program. You can attend meetings and get other benefits, such as people who accept, like, and respect you; good feedback and advice; structure and routine; a safe social circle; and moral and emotional support. However, to have your best chance of staying clean and sober and of being happy and successful in other areas of life, you can't work the 12 steps without Step 3.

Be sure to bring this handout to your next session with your therapist and talk about your thoughts and feelings about the exercise.

# STEP 4: PERSONAL INVENTORY

## GOALS OF THIS EXERCISE

1. Provide a structured format for working Step 4 of a 12-step program.

2. Carry out a self-examination about problems related to addictions.

3. Externalize and solve problems by analyzing thinking errors and dysfunctional relationship patterns.

## SUGGESTIONS FOR PROCESSING THIS EXERCISE WITH CLIENTS

This exercise is designed to guide clients in carrying out this crucial step in any 12-step recovery program. This process is valuable for its effects in increasing clients' insight into their role in creating their own circumstances, internalizing locus of control, and empowerment by understanding the capacity to solve problems by changing attitudes and behaviors. Follow-up would include the exercises devoted to the remaining steps, along with reporting back to the therapist, treatment group, and program sponsor on the outcomes of this exercise.

# STEP 4: PERSONAL INVENTORY

Writing a personal inventory is a frightening and humbling task for many recovering people, but most also report great benefits once they complete this step and Step 5. They feel peace of mind, a strong sense of connection to other people and their Higher Power, and a sense of real progress in their recovery. While you're doing this inventory, don't concern yourself with Step 5. If you have done this step before, discuss what this was like with your 12-step sponsor, your therapist, or someone else in recovery whom you trust.

1. If you are like most people, this step is probably tough for you to carry out. If it's hard for you, what makes it difficult? Why do you feel it is hard for most people?

   _____

   _____

   _____

   _____

2. What benefits do you think writing a "searching and fearless moral inventory" might offer? How could this help a person recover from alcoholism, other chemical dependence, or other addictive behaviors?

   _____

   _____

   _____

   _____

3. Here are the most common reasons people list for this step being hard. Circle any that are true for you:

a.  They feared they would realize they were even worse than they thought they were.

b.  They found remembering old wrongs to be painful, embarrassing, and depressing.

c.  They felt focusing on past problems wouldn't help them change their futures.

d.  When they thought about their whole lives, the task seemed overwhelming and they didn't know how to get started.

4.  Looking at the Big Book and other 12-step literature, you'll find that this step doesn't have to be that hard or complicated. In this exercise, you will use a simple format. The first step is to list resentments. Take a separate piece of paper and divide it into four columns. In the first column, list the people, institutions or organizations, and principles or rules that cause you to feel resentment. Focus on those that cause you to feel resentment when you think of them and write them in the first column. Finish the first column before going on to the second. You'll find a sample worksheet at the end of this exercise. Make as many copies as you need to list all your resentments; most people need several pages.

5.  Now in the second column, for each of the people, institutions, or principles you put in the first column, list what they have done to you or what they might do to cause your resentment. Again, fill this column out completely before moving on to the third column.

6.  People tend to resent anything they think might deprive them of something they want or need. In the third column, list the want or need in your life that these people, institutions, or principles have negatively affected. Choose from the following list:

a.  Self-esteem

b.  Relationships with other people

c.  Emotional security

d.  Physical and material security

e.  Sex life

7.  The Big Book points out that we are often partly at fault in situations where we have resentments. Our wrongs fall into four categories. In the fourth column, for each of these people, institutions, or principles, list anything <u>you</u> have done that has contributed to your problems with each person, institution, or principle. Have you acted in ways that have been selfish, inconsiderate, dishonest, or fearful? Or was your part, perhaps, simply keeping your resentment and self-pity going, nursing these negative feelings and keeping the hurts fresh instead of letting yourself move on?

8.  This is your resentment inventory. Now do the same with fears. Make a similar list of people, institutions, or principles that cause you fear or anxiety. Use the same four columns and fill each column out completely before starting the next. When you complete your inventory related to fears, you may find that it has most of the same names on it as the resentment inventory.

9.  The third part of this "searching and fearless moral inventory" relates to sex. Most alcoholics, addicts, and other compulsive people have had problems with this area of their lives. So for this part, use a separate sheet to list your sexual wrongs. In the first column, again list people, institutions, or principles you have hurt. In the second column list what you did that hurt them. In column three, list what motivated your actions in each case, again choosing from:

    a.  Self-esteem

    b.  Relationships with other people

    c.  Emotional security

    d.  Physical and material security

    e.  Sex life

    Finally, in the fourth column, list the category your wrong actions fit into, choosing from:

    a.  Selfishness

    b.  Dishonesty

    c. Fear

    d. Lack of consideration

10. Finally, remember: A complete inventory includes both good and bad. Take another sheet or sheets of paper and list your strengths and positive qualities and the good things you do in your daily life.

11. You have now done your Step 4 inventory. Don't fall into the trap of working endlessly on your inventory and never finishing it. Do the best you can for now. Later on you will remember other things you left out, and that's okay. Most recovering people do this over every now and then. However, we caution you not to deliberately leave your inventory incomplete. If there are secrets you are afraid to share with anyone, those are the most important things to list.

12. Once you have completed Step 4, it's best to move on to Step 5 as soon as you can. A wise saying in recovery groups is that doing an inventory and not sharing it with someone is like brushing your teeth and not spitting it out—it will soon start feeling worse instead of better. We will address how best to do Step 5 in the next assignment.

Be sure to bring this handout to your next session with your therapist and talk about your thoughts and feelings about the exercise.

# REVIEW OF RESENTMENTS

| I am resentful at (people, institutions, or principles): | What they have done or might do to me: | Caused by my/ affects my: Self-esteem? Relationships with others? Emotional security? Physical/material security? Sex life? | My part—was I: Selfish? Inconsiderate? Dishonest? Fearful? |
|---|---|---|---|
| | | | |
| | | | |
| | | | |
| | | | |
| | | | |
| | | | |
| | | | |
| | | | |
| | | | |
| | | | |
| | | | |
| | | | |
| | | | |
| | | | |
| | | | |
| | | | |
| | | | |
| | | | |
| | | | |
| | | | |

# REVIEW OF FEARS

| I am fearful of (people, institutions, or principles): | What they have done or might do to me: | Caused by my/ affects my:<br><br>Self-esteem?<br>Relationships with others?<br>Emotional security?<br>Physical/material security?<br>Sex life? | My part—was I:<br><br>Selfish?<br>Inconsiderate?<br>Dishonest?<br>Fearful? |
|---|---|---|---|
| | | | |
| | | | |
| | | | |
| | | | |
| | | | |
| | | | |
| | | | |
| | | | |
| | | | |
| | | | |
| | | | |
| | | | |
| | | | |
| | | | |
| | | | |
| | | | |
| | | | |
| | | | |
| | | | |
| | | | |
| | | | |

# REVIEW OF SEXUAL WRONGS

| I have wronged (people, institutions, or principles): | What I did that hurt them: | My actions were motivated by: Self-esteem? Relationships with others? Emotional security? Physical/material security? Sex life? | How I was wrong—was I: Selfish? Inconsiderate? Dishonest? Fearful? |
|---|---|---|---|
| | | | |
| | | | |
| | | | |
| | | | |
| | | | |
| | | | |
| | | | |
| | | | |
| | | | |
| | | | |
| | | | |
| | | | |
| | | | |
| | | | |
| | | | |
| | | | |
| | | | |
| | | | |
| | | | |
| | | | |
| | | | |

# REVIEW OF STRENGTHS AND POSITIVE QUALITIES

| Strength or positive quality: | How it has been demonstrated in my daily life: |
|---|---|
| | |
| | |
| | |
| | |
| | |
| | |
| | |
| | |
| | |
| | |
| | |
| | |
| | |
| | |
| | |
| | |
| | |
| | |
| | |
| | |

# STEP 5: SHARING THE STEP-4 INVENTORY

## GOALS OF THIS EXERCISE

1. Decrease isolation caused by shame and low self-esteem.

2. Increase identification with successful role models who are successfully coping with similar issues.

3. Increase sense of empowerment and efficacy in taking action to resolve personal issues.

## SUGGESTIONS FOR PROCESSING THIS EXERCISE WITH CLIENTS

This exercise is designed to guide clients in sharing the Step-4 inventory with recovery program sponsors or other trustworthy and appropriate figures. It is crucial for its effects in increasing self-acceptance, reducing isolation, and increasing a sense of self-efficacy and affiliation with the recovery program. Follow-up would include the exercises devoted to the remaining steps, along with reporting back to the therapist, treatment group, and program sponsor on the outcomes of this exercise.

# STEP 5: SHARING THE STEP-4 INVENTORY

Many recovering people will report that sharing their personal inventories was frightening before they did it and freeing afterward. As noted in the exercise on Step 4, they describe feeling peace of mind, a stronger connection to others and their Higher Power, and a sense of a major step forward in recovery. If you have done this step before, discuss what this was like with your 12-step sponsor, your therapist, or someone else in recovery whom you trust.

1. Like Step 4, this step is very tough for many people. If it's hard for you, what makes it difficult? Why do you feel Step 5 is hard for most people?

   _____

   _____

   _____

   _____

2. Step 5 is frightening for most of us. If you are worried by the idea of writing an inventory and sharing it with someone else, what are you afraid will happen?

   _____

   _____

   _____

   _____

3. The two greatest fears most people feel are these: We fear that the people who hear our inventories will reject us—that we will lose their respect and friendship—and we fear that they will tell our

secrets to others. Both of these fears are reasonable. To keep these things from happening, it is important to choose the right kind of person to hear the inventory.

Some people you might be able to trust with this could include your sponsor or another person from a 12-step program, a close friend, a doctor or therapist, a priest or minister, or a trusted relative. Choose very carefully. Who might you choose to hear your own inventory?

_____

_____

_____

_____

_____

4. Once you have chosen the person, talk to them and explain what you are doing and what you are asking of them. If they seem understanding and agree to help you by hearing your inventory, choose a time and place where the two of you will have privacy and enough time to read through the inventory and talk about it. Then go and share this inventory with that person.

5. If your experience is like that of most people, the person hearing your inventory will not only accept and respect you, he or she will also have had some of the problems you felt the most fear and shame about revealing. Once you have completed Step 5, sit quietly and notice how your feelings have changed. Most people feel a sense of relief and a new peace of mind, as if a great burden had been lifted from them. They feel less isolated and more connected with others, and many even feel a strong sense of the presence of their Higher Power, maybe for the first time. Please list the feelings or thoughts that come to you:

_____

_____

_____

_____

_____

6. Once you have completed Step 5, you are ready to move on to Step 6, and it's best to do so as soon as you can. We will address this in the next assignment.

Be sure to bring this handout to your next session with your therapist and talk about your thoughts and feelings about the exercise.

# STEP 6: BECOMING WILLING TO CHANGE

## GOALS OF THIS EXERCISE

1. Provide a structured format for working Step 6 of a 12-step program.

2. Increase openness to growth and positive change.

3. Together with Step 7, make positive changes in self-image and interactions with others, replacing dysfunctional patterns identified in Steps 4 and 5 with healthy alternatives.

## SUGGESTIONS FOR PROCESSING THIS EXERCISE WITH CLIENTS

This exercise is designed to guide clients who are carrying out this step and are actively engaged in working a 12-step program. It may also be useful for other clients who are motivated to change and are comfortable working in a spiritually based framework. The exercise guides clients in acknowledging the need for change and thinking about positive aspects of life after giving up dysfunctional behavior patterns. Follow-up would include the exercises devoted to the remaining steps, along with reporting back to the therapist, treatment group, and program sponsor on the outcomes of this activity.

# STEP 6: BECOMING WILLING TO CHANGE

This step and Step 7 are linked to Step 3. In a way, this is where you start to carry out the decision you made in that step to turn your will and your life over to the care of God as you understand God. If you have done this step before, discuss what this was like with your 12-step sponsor, your therapist, or someone else in recovery whom you trust.

1. Step 6 asks you to be "entirely willing" to have God remove your defects of character. Keeping in mind the inventory you wrote and shared in Steps 4 and 5, what does the phrase "defects of character" mean to you? How would you define them?

   _____

   _____

   _____

   _____

2. Looking at the things you listed in your inventory, think about what defects of character you feel led to these actions and situations in your life. You will probably see the same underlying patterns of thinking and feeling, over and over, connected to all the things you listed in your inventory. What are these defects of character in your life?

   _____

   _____

   _____

   _____

3. People often feel they need to keep some of their defects of character because they don't see how they could get along and take care of themselves without them. Do you have behavior patterns that you have depended on to cope with life? What are they?

_____

_____

_____

_____

4. Have you tried to change these patterns before through willpower or intelligence? _____ If you have, how well did that work?

_____

_____

_____

_____

5. This step involves giving up the effort to control and make things happen yourself and trusting your Higher Power that you will be better and will like yourself better after being changed by the removal of these problems. How do you feel about this trust?

_____

_____

_____

_____

6. How would your life be different if these defects of character were removed from you? With what would you want them to be replaced?

_____

_____

_____

_____

7. If you knew you could trust that you could get along in life without these behavior patterns, these defects of character, would you be

willing to give them up? What do you think of the idea of living without these patterns of thinking, feeling, or behavior?

_____

_____

_____

_____

8. If you have tried without success to change through willpower or reasoning, how do you feel about the idea that your Higher Power could remove them where you hadn't been able to? What do you think this experience would be like? Have you talked with your sponsor or other people in recovery you trust and respect about their experiences with Step 6, and if so, what did they say about these things?

_____

_____

_____

_____

Be sure to bring this handout to your next session with your therapist and talk about your thoughts and feelings about the exercise.

# STEP 7: ASKING FOR CHANGE

## GOALS OF THIS EXERCISE

1.  Provide a structured format for working Step 7 of a 12-step program.

2.  Increase commitment to growth and positive behavioral change.

3.  Together with Step 6, make positive changes in self-image and interactions with others, replacing dysfunctional patterns identified in Steps 4 and 5 with healthy alternatives.

## SUGGESTIONS FOR PROCESSING THIS EXERCISE WITH CLIENTS

This exercise is designed to guide clients who are actively engaged in working a 12-step program to carry out this step. It may also be useful for other clients who are motivated to change and are comfortable working in a spiritually based framework. The exercise guides clients in committing to change. Follow-up would include the exercises devoted to the remaining steps, along with reporting back to the therapist, treatment group, and program sponsor on the outcomes of this activity.

# STEP 7: ASKING FOR CHANGE

Just as Step 3 built on Steps 1 and 2, Step 7 is the first action building on Steps 4, 5, and 6, and is a way to carry out the decision you made in Step 3. If you have done this step before, discuss what this was like with your 12-step sponsor, your therapist, or someone else in recovery whom you trust.

1. Step 6 asked you to become willing to have your Higher Power re-move the problem patterns in your thinking, feelings, and behavior that you identified while writing and sharing your inventory in Steps 4 and 5. Are you willing to have these patterns removed from your life? How do you feel about this idea? Do you think it will work?

   _____

   _____

   _____

   _____

2. Once you have become willing to be changed, does it make sense for you to ask your Higher Power to make this change? What do you think of the idea of letting it be done for you instead of trying to do all the work yourself?

   _____

   _____

   _____

   _____

3. What do you think will happen when you carry out Step 7 and ask your Higher Power to remove your defects of character? Recovering people generally report that rather than having their defects of

character disappear, what happens is that they find they now have the ability to keep from acting out their problem patterns. They may still have the kinds of thoughts or feelings they had before, but now they're able to choose not to act on them. Would this be an improvement for you?

_____

_____

_____

4. Recovering people also usually find that the removal of these defects of character or their being given the ability to manage them is temporary and that if they don't keep working on their recovery program they slide back into the old patterns. Are you willing to keep working on your recovery so that you'll keep getting better, even if it's something you have to keep doing from now on?

_____

_____

_____

5. Some people notice an immediate feeling of being different when they work Step 7, such as the instant vanishing of their urges to drink or use. Others say they go through a more gradual change, not noticing a difference right away, but seeing it over days, weeks, or months. Often others notice before we do that we have changed in small ways, such as finding ourselves being more considerate of other drivers in traffic, laughing about situations that used to cause us to feel anger or anxiety, being more patient with our children, and so on. What are changes you would like others to see in your daily actions and feelings as a result of these steps?

_____

_____

_____

Be sure to bring this handout to your next session with your therapist and talk about your thoughts and feelings about the exercise.

# STEP 8: LISTING PEOPLE HARMED

## GOALS OF THIS EXERCISE

1. Provide a structured format for working Step 8 of a 12-step program.

2. Assist in further recognition and acknowledgement of dysfunctional behaviors and their impacts on others.

3. Increase motivation to treat others with consideration.

## SUGGESTIONS FOR PROCESSING THIS EXERCISE WITH CLIENTS

This exercise is designed for clients actively working in 12-step recovery programs, as well as for others whose self-acceptance would be enhanced by taking responsibility for past abusive behavior toward others. Follow-up would include the activity titled Step 9: Making Amends, as well as the other exercises dedicated to the remaining steps and reporting back to the therapist, treatment group, and program sponsor on the outcomes of this exercise.

# STEP 8: LISTING PEOPLE HARMED

Step 8 is another action step and, like Step 4, is best done without worrying about the step that comes right afterward. Step 8 and its companion, Step 9, are the ones that demonstrate the changes we are going though most clearly to other people in our lives, and they're the most complicated steps for most people and may raise some difficult questions. As with the previous steps, if you have already done Step 8, use this worksheet to record your actions, and talk this over with your therapist and your sponsor.

1. Why stir up old problems? That's one of the first thoughts many recovering people have when they first think about this step. Another is, "No way, I'll never do that!" So why should you do what this step asks? There must be good reasons for so many people to engage in it. To help make the purpose and benefits of Step 8 clear, we'll break it down into phrases.

2. The first thing Step 8 asks you to do is to "make a list of all persons we had harmed." In other words, list who you've hurt and describe what you've done to hurt them. Most people find that the lists of people and institutions they resented and feared, which they created in Step 4, make a good starting point for Step 8. So let's start there. Please look again at those lists. On a separate sheet divided into three columns, list any of the people and institutions from your lists of resentments, fears, and sexual wrongs that you have harmed. A definition of harm often used in 12-step programs is "to cause physical, emotional, spiritual, mental, or material loss or difficulty." In the second column, list what you did in each case. Title the third column *What I can do to correct the harms I caused* and leave it blank for now.

3. Now, how do you feel about those people and institutions and how may they feel about you? If you notice any of the same feelings showing up again and again, on your part or the part of those you've hurt, list those feelings here:

_____

_____

_____

_____

4. How would the feelings in these situations be different if you hadn't done the things you did?

_____

_____

_____

_____

5. What benefits do you think you would gain from having made a list of the people and institutions you've harmed? How do you think this will help you stay clean and sober or avoid returning to any other addictive patterns?

_____

_____

_____

_____

6. The next phrase is "and became willing to make amends to them all." Are you willing to do this, or do you find that in some of the situations you have listed, you are unwilling to make these amends? If so, why?

_____

_____

_____

_____

7. Another point may be useful: Remember that Steps 8 and 9 are separate steps. This one isn't asking you to make the amends yet, only to list the people you've hurt and to become willing to make amends. If you feel like holding back because you don't want to face the people you've hurt or the consequences that may come up with Step 9, then you aren't willing yet. You're still in the middle of Step 8. The second part, becoming willing, is what makes it possible to go on to Step 9. Are you now willing? If not, what might help you become willing to go on to Step 9 and start making amends to people you've hurt? Talk about this with your sponsor or other recovering people you trust and respect.

_____

_____

_____

_____

8. Most of us find that we would rather not make some amends. The word _willing_ is the key. It doesn't say we have to want to or that we have to like doing so, only that we must be willing to do it. List some things you are willing to do because they are needed, even though you would prefer not to (examples could be getting a vaccination or paying income taxes):

_____

_____

_____

_____

9. Why are you willing to do these unpleasant things? Why are they necessary?

_____

_____

_____

_____

10. You may have said you are willing to do unpleasant things because the results would be even more unpleasant if you didn't do them. It's the same with these amends. What do you think you have to lose? In what ways could these amends cause problems for you?

    _____

    _____

    _____

    _____

11. Now balance the things you feel you might lose by making amends against the things you will lose if you relapse. Which set of consequences is worse and why?

    _____

    _____

    _____

    _____

12. If you have trouble understanding how failure to make amends might lead to relapse, think about how leaving these things unresolved affects your self-esteem and your level of stress. Talk about this with your sponsor or others you trust and think about how this interferes with your becoming the person you want to be and with the changes you asked your Higher Power to make in you in Step 7. How would leaving amends undone affect you in these areas?

    _____

    _____

    _____

    _____

Be sure to bring this handout to your next session with your therapist and talk about your thoughts and feelings about the exercise.

## AMENDS LIST

| Who I harmed | What I did and how it hurt them | What I can do to correct the harms I caused |
|---|---|---|
|  |  |  |
|  |  |  |
|  |  |  |
|  |  |  |
|  |  |  |
|  |  |  |
|  |  |  |
|  |  |  |
|  |  |  |
|  |  |  |
|  |  |  |
|  |  |  |
|  |  |  |
|  |  |  |
|  |  |  |
|  |  |  |
|  |  |  |
|  |  |  |
|  |  |  |
|  |  |  |

# STEP 9: MAKING AMENDS

## GOALS OF THIS EXERCISE

1. Provide a structured format for working Step 9 of a 12-step program.

2. Settle unresolved interpersonal issues stemming from past dysfunctional behavior.

3. Enhance self-respect through self-directed, positive changes in interpersonal behavior patterns.

## SUGGESTIONS FOR PROCESSING THIS EXERCISE WITH CLIENTS

This exercise is designed for clients actively working in 12-step recovery programs, as well as for others whose self-acceptance would be enhanced by settling unresolved issues resulting from past abusive or neglectful behavior toward others. Caution should be exercised in situations where the actions in this exercise might expose clients to physical abuse or to emotional or other stresses beyond the capacity of their coping resources and abilities. Follow-up would include the activities dedicated to the remaining steps, as well as reporting back to the therapist, treatment group, and program sponsor on the outcomes of this exercise.

# STEP 9: MAKING AMENDS

It is after this step that AA's Big Book talks about the changes often referred to as the Promises, which experienced people tell us have happened in their lives as they worked the steps. Step 9 is the one that demonstrates the changes you are going through most clearly to other people in your life. Like Step 8, this is a complex step, and with this step it is vitally important to have done all the previous steps and to talk this over with your therapist and your sponsor before taking any action.

1. Again, why stir up old problems? Why should you do what this step asks? The short answers are, first, to stay clean and sober, and second, to bring about the Promises. To look at how this works, we'll break this step into phrases as we've done before.

2. The first phrase says you should make "direct amends to such people wherever possible." Turn to the third column on your amends list. For each person or institution put down the action on your part that would make amends for your past actions. Remember the word *direct*. This means that if you have a choice between doing this face to face or by calling or writing a letter, you do it face to face. It is more uncomfortable this way, but the benefits are greater.

3. You may find that some of these amends are impossible to make. Some people on your list may be dead. Some may have moved away, and you might not know how to find them. You might not even know who some of them are. Would you be willing to make these amends if you could? The key is willingness. You may have to wait to make some amends for years, but if you are ready to do so at the first opportunity, you can make this step work for you.

4. Often if you can't make amends to a specific person or institution, you can make amends by changing the way you treat people or institutions in general. For example, a man who had been homeless in his addiction and had spent many days lying on the grass outside a library, frightening away some members of the community because of his appearance and behavior, donated recovery literature to that library in his sobriety.

5. Before taking any action, you need to consider the second part of Step 9: "except when to do so would injure them or others." What are some ways that people could actually be further injured by someone making amends?

_____

_____

_____

_____

6. Answers would include situations where people would be badly hurt by finding out things they didn't know, such as spouses who didn't know about an infidelity. Other people might also be hurt because of other consequences of your amends. Are there amends on your list that would injure someone if you carried them out as you have written them down? What are they?

_____

_____

_____

_____

7. Are there other ways you can make any of those amends without harming anyone? How?

_____

_____

_____

_____

8. Once you've made your list of the amends you can make without hurting anyone, talk it over with your sponsor or therapist or someone else whose judgment you trust and get their advice about how you should approach these people. Here are some guidelines:

    a. Stick to talking about what you have done, not what they may have done to you. Remember, you're cleaning up your act, not theirs.

    b. Don't let yourself be victimized in this process. That's not healthy either.

    c. Keep in mind that you're doing this for your own recovery, and how they react is less important than how you feel afterward. Some people may be rude or ungrateful. As long as you have no expectations of positive reactions, and you're not doing this in a way that causes hurt, that's okay.

    Once you've made your list, crossed out actions that would hurt others and found different ways to make those amends, and gotten the feedback of someone you trust, it's time to start contacting the people on your list, telling them what you're doing, and carrying out your amends. Make as many of these amends as you can before you answer the next question.

9. How do you feel now that you've made whatever amends you can for the time being? Do you feel that this will help you with your recovery from addiction? How does this help?

    _____

    _____

    _____

    _____

Be sure to bring this handout to your next session with your therapist and talk about your thoughts and feelings about the exercise.

# STEP 10: CONTINUED INVENTORY

## GOALS OF THIS EXERCISE

1. Provide motivation and a method for working Step 10 of a 12-step program.

2. Reduce the likelihood of relapse into addiction or addictive behaviors.

3. Implement new cognitive and emotional coping mechanisms in all areas of life.

## SUGGESTIONS FOR PROCESSING THIS EXERCISE WITH CLIENTS

Along with Steps 11 and 12, this exercise is designed as an ongoing addition to the treatment and recovery plan of clients who have completed the first nine steps of any 12-step program. Since the work done in this step is meant to be continued indefinitely, clients should not expect to complete this exercise and stop the activity. Follow-up should include periodic check-ins with the therapist, treatment group, and program sponsor on maintenance and outcomes of the actions taken in this exercise.

# STEP 10: CONTINUED INVENTORY

Step 10 is the first of the three "continued growth steps." Together with Steps 11 and 12, it will help you avoid sliding back into old patterns and to continue growing and getting healthier in all relationships and areas of your life.

1. Unlike the first nine steps, which you can start and finish, this one along with the two that follow describe an ongoing process. In the case of Step 10, what do you think are some reasons for making personal inventory a continuing practice?

   _____

   _____

   _____

   _____

2. The first part of Step 10 says to "continue to take personal inventory." How can you do this in your own life?

   _____

   _____

   _____

   _____

3. The next phrase is "and when we were wrong, promptly admitted it." Why should you do this? How do you think it will it help?

   _____

   _____

   _____

   _____

4. Have you heard your sponsor or others in recovery whom you trust and respect talk about how they practice Step 10? What do they do?

_____

_____

_____

_____

5. The literature of AA and other 12-step programs offers guidance on putting Step 10 into action. Generally, they advise at least a daily review, either first thing in the morning, just before going to sleep, or both, examining your actions for unhealthy motives, dysfunctional patterns of thoughts or feelings, or harm done to others (intentional or not). How would such a daily inventory be useful in your recovery? What would you do when you realized you had hurt someone or acted wrongly?

_____

_____

_____

_____

6. A major benefit of a daily inventory is to catch problems early and make amends promptly. This reduces stress by avoiding the buildup of tensions in your relationships with others. Have you had an experience when you realized you had made a mistake and immediately made amends for it? _____ How did that feel, compared to times when you realized you'd done something wrong but left it hanging for a longer time?

_____

_____

_____

_____

Be sure to bring this handout to your next session with your therapist and talk about your thoughts and feelings about the exercise.

# STEP 11: IMPROVING CONSCIOUS CONTACT

## GOALS OF THIS EXERCISE

1. Provide motivation and a method for working Step 11 of a 12-step program.

2. Reduce the likelihood of relapse into addiction or addictive behaviors.

3. Implement new cognitive and emotional coping mechanisms into all areas of life.

## SUGGESTIONS FOR PROCESSING THIS EXERCISE WITH CLIENTS

Along with Steps 10 and 12, this exercise is designed as an ongoing addition to the treatment and recovery plan of clients who have completed the first nine steps of any 12-step program. These three steps are designed to be practiced indefinitely, and clients should not expect to complete this exercise and stop these activities. Follow-up should include periodic check-ins with the therapist, treatment group, and program sponsor on maintenance and outcomes of the actions taken in this activity.

# STEP 11: IMPROVING CONSCIOUS CONTACT

Step 11 is one of the three "continued growth steps," falling between Step 10, Continued Inventory, and Step 12, Carrying the Message and Practicing the Principles. This step is designed to be part of the foundation of a daily practice to keep making your recovery stronger and helping you make your life better.

1. In Step 11 you are asked to seek through prayer and meditation to improve your "conscious contact with God as you understand God." How can you do this?

   _____

   _____

   _____

   _____

2. If you're uncomfortable with prayer and meditation or feel you don't know how to do them, who can you ask for guidance on this?

   _____

   _____

   _____

   _____

3. What does "conscious contact with God as you understand God" mean to you?

   _____

   _____

   _____

   _____

4. If you recall some of the questions you answered about Step 3, they talked about different ways your Higher Power might be communicating with you. What ideas did you find worked best for you and can you see ways this communication could be made clearer?

_____

_____

_____

_____

5. How would clearer contact and communication with the God or Higher Power of your understanding help you in your day-to-day life?

_____

_____

_____

_____

6. How can you use prayer or meditation to improve your ability to be aware of and understand this communication or "conscious contact"? How can you do this in your daily life?

_____

_____

_____

_____

7. The second part of Step 11 guides you to pray only for knowledge of God's will for you and the power to carry that out. Why do you think this is written this way, instead of telling you to figure out what's best for you and pray for that to happen?

_____

_____

_____

_____

8. When you were drinking, using, or engaged in other addictive be-haviors, did you make mistakes about what was best for you and what needed to happen in your life? _____ Are you immune from that type of mistaken thinking now, or do you still catch yourself making mistakes in this area? If you still make mistakes like this, please give an example.

_____

_____

_____

_____

9. How can you become more aware of what your God or Higher Power is trying to guide you toward in your life? Do you think that inner voice, or gut feeling, or conscience the Step 3 assignment talked about earlier could be a good guide? _____ How could you be sure you were really following the guidance of your Higher Power instead of your own addictive thinking patterns? Would talking with others about your thoughts help? _____ Who would be the best people to talk with about this?

_____

_____

_____

_____

10. The last part of Step 11 asks for the "power to carry that out." How could your God or Higher Power help in this area?

_____

_____

_____

_____

Be sure to bring this handout to your next session with your therapist and talk about your thoughts and feelings about the exercise.

# STEP 12: CARRYING THE MESSAGE

## GOALS OF THIS EXERCISE

1. Provide motivation and guidance for working Step 12 of a 12-step program.

2. Reduce the likelihood of relapse into addiction or addictive behaviors.

3. Implement new cognitive and emotional coping mechanisms into all areas of life.

4. Increase self-esteem and affiliation with a positive peer groups.

## SUGGESTIONS FOR PROCESSING THIS EXERCISE WITH CLIENTS

Together with Steps 10 and 11, this exercise is designed as an ongoing addition to the treatment and recovery plan of clients who have completed the first nine steps of any 12-step program. These steps are planned as lifelong practices, so clients should not expect to complete this exercise and stop these activities. Follow-up should include periodic check-ins with the therapist, treatment group, and program sponsor on maintenance and outcomes of the actions taken in this activity.

# STEP 12: CARRYING THE MESSAGE

Step 12 is the last step, but counter to what people often think when they start a 12-step program, the steps are never finished. Along with Steps 10 and 11, this is one of the "continued growth" steps.

1. Step 12 starts out, "Having had a spiritual awakening as the result of these Steps, . . ." Do you feel you've had a spiritual awakening? _____ What does this phrase mean to you?

   _____

   _____

   _____

   _____

2. Some people say that "a spiritual awakening" is another way of saying "a change of attitude." Have you had a change of attitude? _____ If so, how would you describe this change?

   _____

   _____

   _____

   _____

3. Do you feel that your spiritual awakening or change of attitude is "the result of these steps"? _____ If so, how have the steps changed you?

   _____

   _____

   _____

   _____

4. The next part of Step 12 says that we are to try to "carry this message" to others, either alcoholics if we are involved in AA, addicts if our program is NA, or others with other programs. This can be anyone who has the same problems we have overcome. How can you do this, and how much are you doing so now?

_____

_____

_____

5. What benefits do you get from doing this? How does it help you in your recovery?

_____

_____

_____

_____

6. The final part of Step 12 says that we "practice these principles in all our affairs" or, in some programs, "in all areas of our lives." What does this mean to you?

_____

_____

_____

7. How will you carry out this part of Step 12 in your own daily life?

_____

_____

_____

8. What benefits do you expect to get from "practicing these principles in all your affairs"? Why should you do this, and how will it help you in your recovery?

_____

_____

_____

At this point, if you continue to practice Steps 10 through 12, you have worked your way through the steps and are continuing to use a system that has helped millions of people avoid relapse and continue to grow in peace of mind and the ability to handle life's difficulties. If you are actively practicing your program, you have a support group of people who know you, accept you, and care what happens to you. You are also a support to others and are growing in the ability to be the person you wish to be.

To conclude this series of worksheets, we will review the "Promises," which the Big Book tells you that you can expect to come true for you if you continue to work at this:

> If we are painstaking about this phase of our development, we will be amazed before we are halfway through. We are going to know a new freedom and a new happiness. We will not regret the past nor wish to shut the door on it. We will comprehend the word serenity and we will know peace. No matter how far down the scale we have gone, we will see how our experience can benefit others. That feeling of uselessness and self-pity will disappear. We will lose interest in selfish things and gain interest in our fellows. Self-seeking will slip away. Our whole attitude and outlook upon life will change. Fear of people and of economic insecurity will leave us. We will intuitively know how to handle situations which used to baffle us. We will suddenly realize that God is doing for us what we could not do for ourselves. (*Alcoholics Anonymous*, pp. 83–84)

Be sure to bring this handout to your next session with your therapist and talk about your thoughts and feelings about the exercise.

# SPECIAL-OCCASION RELAPSE PREVENTION IN 12-STEP RECOVERY

## GOALS OF THIS EXERCISE

1. Prompt planning to cope with situations that might otherwise trigger relapses.

2. Provide guidance in planning the use of 12-step recovery resources for stressful situations.

3. Provide guidance in creating a structured plan for using 12-step resources to avoid relapse in difficult situations.

## SUGGESTIONS FOR PROCESSING THIS EXERCISE WITH CLIENTS

This exercise is designed for clients in early recovery to provide both a concrete plan for avoiding relapse in challenging situations and a greater awareness of ways they can systematically use 12-step resources and recovery program strategies to remain abstinent. Follow-up should include reviewing the assignment when the client has answered the questions and drafted his or her plans and periodic check-ins to see whether the client has used all or part of the plan and whether it was effective.

# SPECIAL-OCCASION RELAPSE PREVENTION IN 12-STEP RECOVERY

Some situations make it harder than usual to stay clean, sober, and abstinent from addiction. This may be true about celebrations, such as weddings and holidays, crises such as deaths of loved ones or major financial setbacks, or just difficult situations that make it harder to use the recovery tools you would normally use, such as when you're traveling. These situations are out of the daily routine, but at the same time they're part of a normal life. Dealing with unexpected, uncomfortable, and stressful life events is inevitable. You'll have to handle tough situations the rest of your life. Some difficult situations are avoidable and some aren't, but they can all be managed without returning to addictive behaviors.

Special occasions and crises often leave people feeling overwhelmed by stress, and addictive behavior is often the first response that comes to mind for a long time after getting clean and sober. Further, mood swings are a part of early recovery, and they can make stressful situations feel more challenging than they normally would. This exercise will help you plan today, before the challenging special occasions, so you can avoid or cope with crisis and use the tools of your 12-step recovery program to avoid relapse.

Some special occasions are predictable, inevitable, and recurring, such as holidays and birthdays. Others are less regular but still known in advance, such as weddings and christenings. There will be some happy occasions that take you by surprise, but you can plan for them. Of the more painful types of special occasions, some crises are not surprises, and some seem to come out of nowhere. Crises can be external (related to other people's situations and actions) or internal (related to your own changes as you go through life and recovery).

This means that every recovering person needs to plan ways to use the tools of his or her recovery program for both kinds of stressful situations, those he or she can see coming and those that are surprises.

1. Use this space to write about the recovery tools you will use to cope with special occasions that might make it harder than usual for you to stay abstinent.

   a. How will you use the steps of your program? Write about how you will apply them, especially Steps 1 through 3, when faced with a challenge to your recovery.

_____
_____
_____
_____
_____
_____

   b. How will you use your relationship with your sponsor?

_____
_____
_____
_____
_____
_____

   c. How will you handle being unable to go to your home group or other meetings you usually attend?

_____
_____
_____
_____
_____
_____

2. It's wise to make specific plans for the tough situations you can see coming. What holidays or other regular events or situations are especially hard for you to get through without falling back into addictive behaviors?

_____

_____

_____

3. Here are a dozen common methods people in recovery use for situations like these. Please list the situations you named for question 2 in the following grid, then mark off the methods that would work for you in those situations:

   a. Don't go if you don't have to and don't feel safe.

   b. Make a short appearance and leave quickly.

   c. Make sure you're rested and feeling okay physically.

   d. Take your own vehicle and leave if you feel shaky.

   e. Ask supportive friends or family who will be there to help you avoid relapse.

   f. Let your sponsor or other recovering friends know where you're going and make arrangements to call them when you leave the event or situation and tell them about it.

   g. For a holiday, check with local 12-step meeting clubs to see whether any marathon meetings or other sober social events are planned and, if they are, plan your day around them.

   h. Take a recovering friend along to keep you company.

   i. Go to extra meetings before the event or situation.

   j. Use extra prayer and meditation ahead of time.

   k. Talk about your concerns at a meeting before the event.

   l. Keep phone numbers of recovering friends and a cell phone with you.

   m. Call the local central office and go to meetings wherever you travel.

| Stressful Occasions | Methods to Avoid Relapse | | | | | | | | | | | |
|---|---|---|---|---|---|---|---|---|---|---|---|---|
| | a | b | c | d | e | f | g | h | i | j | k | l |
| | a | b | c | d | e | f | g | h | i | j | k | l |
| | a | b | c | d | e | f | g | h | i | j | k | l |
| | a | b | c | d | e | f | g | h | i | j | k | l |
| | a | b | c | d | e | f | g | h | i | j | k | l |
| | a | b | c | d | e | f | g | h | i | j | k | l |

4. Now take the information you've written down in this exercise and write out a simple plan for handling a special occasion that causes you a lot of stress and makes it hard for you to stay clean and sober from your addiction. Talk this assignment over with your sponsor, and once you've written your plan review it with him or her, as well as with your therapist or counselor, and make improvements in the plan if you get new ideas from them. Once you've done this, keep the plan in your wallet or purse so that you'll have it with you if you need it unexpectedly.

# USING 12-STEP LITERATURE

## GOALS OF THIS EXERCISE

1. Gain awareness of 12-step program literature available as a resource for recovery.

2. Begin effective use of 12-step program literature.

3. Gain insight into answers and solutions to specific questions and issues forming personal obstacles to recovery.

4. Increase step-focused interaction with a sponsor and other 12-step program members.

## SUGGESTIONS FOR PROCESSING THIS EXERCISE WITH CLIENTS

The exercise is designed for clients in early recovery to enhance engagement in step-oriented work and to address any specific issues that may impede the clients' recovery. Greater time should be allowed for this assignment than for others because it requires more reading and discussion and may require clients to order literature they do not have access to. Follow-up should include asking the client about progress or problems with this assignment at each contact before the assignment is due and a review by the therapist of the literature the client is reading. Once the initial part of the assignment is done, the therapist should continue to regularly raise the topic of the use of program literature and ensure that the client is continuing to make this part of his or her recovery program.

# USING 12-STEP LITERATURE

One of the most important resources people in 12-step recovery use to stay clean, sober, and abstinent from their other addictive behaviors is the literature of the programs. Meetings are vital, working the steps is critical, and sponsorship is equally valuable, but without the literature these other resources can't be used with full effectiveness.

Most of the larger 12-step programs have their own Big Books. These books have been published by Alcoholics Anonymous, Cocaine Anonymous, Codependents Anonymous, Debtors Anonymous, Emotions Anonymous, Gamblers Anonymous, Narcotics Anonymous, Overeaters Anonymous, Recovering Couples Anonymous, Sex and Love Addicts Anonymous, and Al-Anon. More are being published. These books describe the addictions their parent programs exist to overcome, relate the history of the programs' creation and growth, talk about how the programs work, and tell the stories of typical members of the programs.

In addition to these primary books, several programs have published additional volumes about their use of the 12 Steps and 12 Traditions.

If you are like most people working to recover from any addiction, you will find ideas and information you can use in any or all of these books, whether or not they are about your particular program(s). There are also many books about various aspects of recovery that apply to issues that come up in all 12-step recovery programs, such as finding a Higher Power and working the steps.

Finally, there are numerous pamphlets on various subjects, and there are magazines such as AA's monthly *Grapevine* containing articles, discussion, and information about recovery conferences, conventions, and other events.

You can get all this literature in several ways: Mainstream bookstores may carry some titles, recovery bookstores will have extensive inventories, most programs sell their literature by mail, and you may be able to order by phone or through Internet web sites.

1. Do you have a copy of the primary book for the recovery program in which you participate? _____ If not, the next step in this assignment is to get a copy, then proceed with question 2. If you are participating in a program that doesn't have such a book, you may want to get the book *Narcotics Anonymous* and use it, because it does a good job of addressing addictive behavior in general. Substitute your own addictive behavior where it talks about using drugs.

2. Read or reread the introductory section(s) in the book. Highlight or underline whatever sentences or phrases in the introduction seem most important, most confusing, or hardest for you to agree with. If you have questions or comments, write them in the margins. Once you've done this, go back and reread the parts you marked. Look for common themes related to things you have trouble understanding or accepting. For example, some people have a hard time accepting the idea that their addiction is a disease, and others can't really believe there's no way they can control it with their own willpower and knowledge. What common themes do you see?

   _____

   _____

   _____

3. In addition to the things you noted in question 2 that confuse or bother you about what you've read, are there other problems or issues in your life that you think might interfere with your ability to participate fully in this recovery program? For example, do you feel less able to fit in because you are different from most of the people in your meetings, or does your situation seem different than those of most people? If so, list these additional issues here.

   _____

   _____

   _____

4. If your group has other books or pamphlets available, see whether they address any questions or problems you listed for questions 2 and 3 of this exercise. For example, there may be material about special concerns of women, younger people, older people, gay or lesbian people, members of minorities, people struggling with the idea of a higher power, people in the military, people in prison, people who need to take medications for other conditions, or those in other situations. If your program has a central office in your area or has a web site where you can get materials, check with those sources too. Get whatever materials you can find and read them. Do they help you with the things that you wrote about?

_____

_____

_____

_____

5. Talk with your sponsor and other experienced people you trust in your recovery group about the items you marked in your book, and what you've found out from other literature. Ask them to share their experience and knowledge with you and to tell you about any more books or literature that might be useful, including other sections of the book you started with, especially any stories of others who've had the same problems or questions. What did you learn from them and from any new material they shared with you?

_____

_____

_____

_____

6. Talk with your sponsor again and make a plan to keep reading your program's primary book or the other book you've used for this exercise, at whatever pace you can. It's important to read often, highlight or underline where you have questions or disagreements, add comments in the margins, and talk about what you've read with your sponsor and your counselor or therapist. Make a schedule with your sponsor, in writing. How often will you read parts of your

book and talk them over with your sponsor and your counselor or therapist?

_____

_____

_____

_____

7. What other books or literature will you read and study after you finish reading the first book you're working on?

_____

_____

_____

_____

Be sure to bring this handout to your next session with your therapist and talk about your answers on this assignment.

# 12-STEP RECOVERY ISSUES FOR YOUNG PEOPLE

## GOALS OF THIS EXERCISE

1. Enable greater identification and affiliation with others participating in 12-step programs.

2. Identify and use 12-step program literature relevant to young people's issues in recovery.

3. Increase step-focused interactions with peers and other 12-step program members.

## SUGGESTIONS FOR PROCESSING THIS EXERCISE WITH CLIENTS

This exercise is designed for youthful clients in early recovery who experience difficulty identifying and affiliating with their 12-step groups because of age differences between themselves and other members. Greater time should be allowed for this assignment than for others because it requires more reading and discussion and may require clients to order literature they do not have access to. Follow-up should include asking the client about progress or problems with this assignment at each contact before the assignment is due and a review by the therapist of the literature the client is reading. Once the initial part of the assignment is done, the therapist should continue to periodically raise the topic of participation in young people's groups or conferences and encourage the client to make this part of his or her recovery program.

# 12-STEP RECOVERY ISSUES FOR YOUNG PEOPLE

Do you sometimes feel out of place in 12-step group meetings because most of the people there are older than you are and seem to have a different set of problems and interests? You might have a hard time believing or accepting that someone as young as you are could be an addict or alcoholic, since you haven't been using, drinking, or engaged in other addictive behaviors as long as most of the people you see. You may not have the high tolerance for alcohol or another drug that some people describe, and you have probably not had many of the losses and painful experiences they talk about, such as divorce, bankruptcy, major medical problems, going to jail or prison, and so on.

You may also find that some people don't take your situation seriously or don't believe you could be an addict or alcoholic because you are young. If so, you aren't alone. Many others have had the same experience in the past or are dealing with it now. This assignment will give you some pointers in getting past this obstacle so you can feel at home in meetings and get the full benefit of the support and experience of others in your recovery.

1. Have you read any of the stories in the back sections of the Big Books used by different 12-step programs? Some of the authors entered recovery while they were young and have written about their experiences. Some of them succeeded in staying clean and sober at that point and others returned to their addictive behaviors until they hit bottom some time later. Examples include the following:

   a. In *Alcoholics Anonymous,* 4th edition, the stories titled "The Missing Link," "My Chance to Live," "Window of Opportunity," and "Freedom from Bondage" all relate the experiences of people who hit bottom while young and found ways to use the tools of that program to stay sober.

b. In the book *Narcotics Anonymous*, read the stories titled "A Gift Called Life," "It's Okay to Be Clean," "How Do You Spell Relief," "Pothead!" "Early Services," "It Won't Get Any Worse," "No Excuse for Loneliness," and "Sick and Tired at Eighteen."

c. *Hope, Faith, and Courage: Stories from the Fellowship of Cocaine Anonymous* includes stories by young people titled "To Be the Best," "Happy, Joyous and Free . . . Finally," "A Lesbian Gets Clean and Sober," "A Stranger in the Mirror," and "Living for the Moment."

d. In *Overeaters Anonymous*, stories by people who attended their first meetings young include "It Wasn't Fair," "Something Dependable," and "Beyond Affliction."

2. Choose at least one of these books and read the stories listed. What do you have in common with the authors of the stories you read?

_____

_____

_____

_____

3. In addition to the stories in the books, other recovery program literature may help you. Check with your meeting's literature representative, your program's nearest central office, and any web sites that may feature your program's literature and get copies of any pamphlets that address special issues or questions of young people. One example is a pamphlet published by the Alcoholic Anonymous General Service Office titled "Young People and AA." Were you able to find any pieces of literature written for young people? _____ If so, were they helpful, and what information was useful to you?

_____

_____

_____

_____

4. Many other people in recovery have had to find solutions to the same problem. One way to find out what has worked for them is to ask them directly. Find at least three people in your recovery program who were about your age when they got clean and sober, and ask them how they dealt with the feelings of not fitting in because of their age. After doing this, what useful feedback did these people give you?

_____

_____

_____

_____

_____

_____

5. Another way to get the benefit of others' experiences is to bring the subject up as a topic at a discussion meeting. Choose a meeting, then bring up this topic. You can do this by talking with the chairperson before the meeting and asking him or her to make it the topic, or you can share your own difficulty with it during a meeting and ask for others to give you their feedback either during or after the meeting. After doing this, what did you find out?

_____

_____

_____

_____

_____

_____

6. Last but not least, your program may have some young people's meetings in your area, and some programs hold regular conferences for young people. Use a meeting schedule and contact your nearest central office to find out when and where any young people's groups meet and about any upcoming young people's conferences. Once you've located some young people's meetings or conferences, try attending them and see whether you feel more comfortable there than at other meetings. How was your experience at a young people's

meeting or conference different from your experiences in other re-covery settings?

_____

_____

_____

_____

Be sure to bring this handout to your next session with your therapist and talk about your answers on this assignment.

# 12-STEP RECOVERY ISSUES FOR WOMEN

## GOALS OF THIS EXERCISE

1. Enable greater identification and affiliation with others participating in 12-step programs.

2. Identify and use 12-step program literature relevant to women's issues in recovery.

3. Increase step-focused interactions with peers and other 12-step program members.

## SUGGESTIONS FOR PROCESSING THIS EXERCISE WITH CLIENTS

This exercise is designed for female clients in early recovery who experience difficulty identifying and affiliating with their 12-step groups because they find that most members they encounter are male or who have difficulty because of negative interactions with some men in recovery groups. Greater time should be allowed for this assignment than for others because it requires more reading and discussion and may require clients to order literature they do not have access to. Follow-up should include asking the client about progress or problems with this assignment at each contact before the assignment is due and a review by the therapist of the literature the client is reading. Once the initial part of the assignment is done, the therapist should continue to periodically raise the topic of participation in women's groups or conferences and encourage the client to make this part of her recovery program.

# 12-STEP RECOVERY ISSUES FOR WOMEN

Do you sometimes feel conspicuous or uncomfortable in the 12-step group meetings you've attended because most of the people there are male and seem to have a different set of problems and interests? You might also have found yourself the object of unwelcome attention from some men at meetings.

You may have learned from an early age that although it is unfair, there are different standards for men and for women. In our society, many believe that addictive behavior, especially drinking, is more acceptable for men than for women. You might have found less understanding and support if you tried to talk with family or friends about your problems and your feelings about them. For these reasons more women than men are solitary and secretive in their addictive practices and have a harder time opening up and letting anyone else know about their secret lives.

If these thoughts and feelings sound familiar, you aren't alone. Many women have had the same experiences in the past and are dealing with them now. This assignment will give you some tips on getting past these obstacles so you can feel at home in meetings and get the full benefit of the support and experience of others in your recovery.

1. Have you read any of the stories in the back sections of the Big Books used by different 12-step programs? Many of the authors are women, too many to list here. Choose the book related to your recovery program and some other books if you like.

2.  Find and read some of the stories by women. What do you have in common with the authors of the stories you read?

    _____

    _____

    _____

    _____

    _____

3.  In addition to the stories in the books, other recovery program literature may help you. Check with your meeting's literature representative, your program's nearest central office, and any web sites that may feature your program's literature and get copies of any pamphlets that address special issues or questions of women in recovery. An example is a pamphlet published by the Alcoholics Anonymous General Service Office titled "AA for the Woman." Were you able to find any recovery literature for women? _____
    If so, was it helpful, and what information was useful to you?

    _____

    _____

    _____

    _____

    _____

4.  Some of the literature, especially in AA, can seem very male-oriented, from referring to the alcoholic or addict as "he" and "him" throughout to referring to God as male. Is this something that makes it more difficult for you to relate to your recovery program and make use of its tools? _____ If it is, try this: Take a chapter of a book or a prayer in which this male-oriented language is an obstacle for you and read through it aloud substituting female pronouns for male—replace "he" with "she," "him" with "her," and so on. Does this make it seem more useful and relevant to you? _____ If so, you can keep doing this when you use program literature in your recovery work.

5. Many other women in recovery have had to find solutions to the same problems. One way to find out what has worked for them is to ask them directly. Find at least three women in your recovery program who strike you as having the quality of sobriety and recovery you would like to have and ask them how they dealt with any problems of not fitting in because of their gender. After doing this, what useful feedback did these people give you?

_____

_____

_____

_____

_____

6. Another way to get the benefit of others' experiences is to bring the subject up as a topic at a discussion meeting. Choose a meeting, then bring up this topic. You can do this by talking with the chair-person before the meeting and asking him or her to make it the topic, or you can share your own difficulty with it during a meeting and ask for others to give you their feedback either during or after the meeting. After doing this, what did you find out?

_____

_____

_____

_____

_____

7. Last but not least, your program may have some women's meetings in your area, and some programs hold regular conferences for women in recovery. Use a meeting schedule and contact your nearest central office to find out when and where any women's groups meet and about any upcoming women's conferences (*note:* If there aren't any, maybe it would be a good idea to talk with some women experienced in sobriety about starting a women's group). Once you've located some of these meetings or conferences, try attending them and see whether you feel more comfortable there than at other meetings. How was your experience at a women's meeting or

conference different from your experiences in other recovery settings?

_____

_____

_____

_____

_____

Be sure to bring this handout to your next session with your therapist and talk about your answers on this assignment.

# 12-STEP RECOVERY ISSUES FOR GAY-LESBIAN-BISEXUAL-TRANSGENDERED PEOPLE

## GOALS OF THIS EXERCISE

1. Enable greater identification and affiliation with others participating in 12-step programs.

2. Identify and use 12-step program literature relevant to gay-lesbian-bisexual-transgendered (GLBT) people's issues in recovery.

3. Increase step-focused interactions with peers and other 12-step program members.

## SUGGESTIONS FOR PROCESSING THIS EXERCISE WITH CLIENTS

This exercise is designed for GLBT clients in early recovery who experience difficulty identifying and affiliating with their 12-step groups because they encounter homophobic attitudes among members of those groups or who have difficulty fitting into social activities in their groups because of their gender orientation or identity. Greater time should be allowed for this assignment than for others because it requires more reading and discussion and may require clients to order literature they do not have access to. Follow-up should include asking the client about progress or problems with this assignment at each contact before the assignment is due and a review by the therapist of the literature the client is reading. Once the initial part of the assignment is done, the therapist should continue to periodically raise the topic of participation in GLBT groups and encourage the client to make this part of his or her recovery program.

# 12-STEP RECOVERY ISSUES FOR GAY-LESBIAN-BISEXUAL-TRANSGENDERED PEOPLE

Do you sometimes feel that you don't fit in the 12-step group meetings you've attended because you encounter the same prejudices and biases you've met in other settings, whether or not the people there realized your orientation was different from theirs? You may have heard hurtful or offensive things said, either in meetings or in casual conversations before or after the meetings. You may have found that much of the program literature assumes the reader is heterosexual.

If you've had experiences like these, you are not alone. Many others have had the same experiences in the past and are dealing with them now. This assignment will give you some tips on getting past these obstacles so you can feel at home in meetings and get the full benefit of the support and experience of others in your recovery.

1. Have you read any of the stories in the back sections of the Big Books used by different 12-step programs? Some of the authors are gay or lesbian. Here are some stories to look for:

   a. In *Alcoholics Anonymous,* 4th edition, the author of "Tightrope" describes his experience as a gay man entering that fellowship and finding comfort and acceptance.

   b. *Hope, Faith, and Courage: Stories from the Fellowship of Cocaine Anonymous* includes the story "A Lesbian Gets Clean and Sober."

   c. In *Co-Dependents Anonymous*, you may relate to the story "Tap Dancer No More."

   d. From the book *Sex and Love Addicts Anonymous*, helpful stories include "There's Everything to Look Forward To," "And in the

Meantime, I Get to Have My Life," "Thank You, God, for What You've Given Me," and "An Unmerited Gift."

2. Choose the book related to your recovery program and some other books if you like and read the stories mentioned. What do you have in common with the authors of the stories you read?

_____

_____

_____

_____

3. In addition to the stories in the books, other recovery program literature may help you. Check with your meeting's literature representative, your program's nearest central office, and any web sites that may feature your program's literature and get copies of any pamphlets that address special issues or questions of GLBT people in recovery. An example is the pamphlet published by the Alcoholics Anonymous General Service Office titled "AA and the Gay/ Lesbian Alcoholic." Were you able to find any? _____ If so, were they helpful, and what information was useful to you?

_____

_____

_____

_____

4. Some of the literature, especially in AA, can seem not only heterosexual but very traditionally male-oriented, from referring to the alcoholic or addict as "he" and "him" throughout to referring to God as male. Is this something that makes it more difficult for you to relate to your recovery program and make use of its tools? _____ If it is, try this: Take a chapter of a book or a prayer in which this male-oriented language is an obstacle for you and read through it aloud substituting neutral or female pronouns for male—replace "he" with "it" or "she," "him" with "it" or "her," and so on. Does this make it seem more useful and relevant to you? _____ If so, you can keep doing this when you use program literature in your recovery work.

5. Many other GLBT people in recovery have had to find solutions to the same problems. One way to find out what has worked for them is to ask them directly. Find a person you identify with in your recovery program who strikes you as having the quality of sobriety and recovery you would like to have and ask that person how he or she dealt with any problems of not fitting in because of sexual orientation or identity. After doing this, what useful feedback did this person give you?

_____

_____

_____

_____

6. Last but not least, your program may have some GLBT meetings in your area. Use a meeting schedule and contact your nearest central office to find out when and where any of these groups meet (*note:* If there aren't any, maybe it would be a good idea to talk with some GLBT people experienced in sobriety about starting a group). Once you've located a meeting or meetings, see whether you feel more comfortable there than at other meetings. How was your experience different from your experiences in other recovery settings?

_____

_____

_____

_____

Be sure to bring this handout to your next session with your therapist and talk about your answers on this assignment.

# 12-STEP RECOVERY ISSUES FOR PEOPLE OF NON-CHRISTIAN FAITHS

## GOALS OF THIS EXERCISE

1. Enable greater identification and affiliation with others participating in 12-step programs.

2. Identify and use 12-step program literature relevant to the needs of recovering people who do not identify themselves as Christian.

3. Increase step-focused interactions with peers and other 12-step program members.

## SUGGESTIONS FOR PROCESSING THIS EXERCISE WITH CLIENTS

This exercise is designed for Jewish, Moslem, Native American, Hindu, Buddhist, and other non-Christian clients in early recovery who experience difficulty identifying and affiliating with their 12-step groups because much of the literature and language is couched in traditional Christian terms. Greater time should be allowed for this assignment than for others because it requires more reading and discussion and may require clients to order literature they do not have access to. Follow-up should include asking the client about progress or problems with this assignment at each contact before the assignment is due and a review by the therapist of the literature the client is reading. Once the initial part of the assignment is done, the therapist should continue to periodically raise the topic of participation in recovery groups devoted to the client's faith community, if such groups are available, and encourage the client to make this part of his or her recovery program.

# 12-STEP RECOVERY ISSUES FOR PEOPLE OF NON-CHRISTIAN FAITHS

At first, many people find the emphasis on God in 12-step programs unsettling. For some this is because they have objections to religion in general, while for others, the problem is not the idea of religion but that so much of the language used in program writings and meetings has a Christian orientation. If this doesn't fit with your religious beliefs it may seem like a barrier to you. However, 12-step programs are successfully used all over the world, by people of all faiths and none. The key is the phrase that is emphasized in Steps 3 and 11, telling us that we must have a relationship with a power greater than ourselves, termed *God* in those steps, "as we understand that God or Higher Power." In practical terms, that means that when a specific phrase or prayer doesn't fit for you, the best way to handle it is to talk about it with your sponsor and look for ways to adapt it to your own beliefs.

1. Have you read any of the stories in the back sections of the Big Books used by different 12-step programs? Some of the authors are members of non-Christian faith communities. Here are some stories to look for:

   a. In *Alcoholics Anonymous,* 4th edition, the story titled "A Drunk Like You" relates the experience of a Jewish man who found ways to adapt the parts of that program that were phrased in Christian terms to fit his own faith.

   b. In the book *Hope, Faith, and Courage: Stories from the Fellowship of Cocaine Anonymous*, you may find the story "Save a Prayer" helpful.

   c. In *Overeaters Anonymous*, the story "Program of Suicide Prevention" relates the experience of how a person for whom Christianity was uncomfortable adapted to that recovery program.

2. Choose the book related to your recovery program and some other books if you like and read the stories mentioned. What do you have in common with the authors of the stories you read?

_____

_____

_____

_____

3. Some of the literature, especially in AA, can seem not only Christian but very traditionally male-oriented, from referring to the alcoholic or addict as "he" and "him" throughout to referring to God as male. Is this something that makes it more difficult for you to relate to your recovery program and make use of its tools? _____ If it is, try this: Take a chapter of a book or a prayer in which this male-oriented language is an obstacle for you and read through it aloud substituting neutral or female pronouns for male. Replace "He" or "Him" with whatever term you use for your Higher Power, "he" with "it" or "she," "him" with "it" or "her," and so on. Does this make it seem more useful and relevant to you? _____ If so you can keep doing this when you use program literature in your recovery work.

4. Many other non-Christian people in recovery have had to find solutions to the same problems. One way to find out what has worked for them is to ask them directly. Find a person you identify with in your recovery program who strikes you as having the quality of sobriety and recovery you would like to have and ask that person how he or she dealt with any problems of feeling like an outsider because of belonging to a different faith community. After doing this, what useful feedback did this person give you?

_____

_____

_____

_____

5. Finally, your program may have some meetings in your area for your faith community. Use a meeting schedule and contact your

nearest central office to find out when and where any of these groups meet (*note:* If there aren't any, maybe it would be a good idea to talk with some others experienced in sobriety about starting a group). Once you've located a meeting or meetings, see whether you feel more comfortable there than at other meetings. How was your experience different from your experiences in other recovery settings?

_____

_____

_____

_____

Be sure to bring this handout to your next session with your therapist and talk about your thoughts and feelings about the exercise.

# 12-STEP RECOVERY ISSUES FOR MEMBERS OF MINORITIES

## GOALS OF THIS EXERCISE

1. Enable greater identification and affiliation with others participating in 12-step programs.

2. Identify and use 12-step program literature relevant to the needs of recovering people who do not belong to the majority socioethnic group of the community.

3. Increase step-focused interactions with peers and other 12-step program members.

## SUGGESTIONS FOR PROCESSING THIS EXERCISE WITH CLIENTS

This exercise is designed for Black, Hispanic, Native American, Asian, and other minority clients in early recovery who experience difficulty identifying and affiliating with their 12-step groups because most of the membership of their groups are not members of their minority group. Greater time should be allowed for this assignment than for others because it requires more reading and discussion and may require clients to order literature they do not have access to. Follow-up should include asking the client about progress or problems with this assignment at each contact before the assignment is due and a review by the therapist of the literature the client is reading. Once the initial part of the assignment is done, the therapist should continue to periodically raise the topic of participation in recovery groups devoted to the client's minority community, if such groups are available, and encourage the client to make this part of his or her recovery program.

# 12-STEP RECOVERY ISSUES FOR MEMBERS OF MINORITIES

Members of minorities often find 12-step meetings uncomfortable, especially when everyone else in the room may look or sound different. However, as it says in Chapter 2 of the book *Alcoholics Anonymous,* "We are people who normally would not mix. But there exists among us a fellowship, a friendliness, and an understanding which is indescribably wonderful. . . . The tremendous fact for every one of us is that we have discovered a common solution." (Alcoholics Anonymous, p. 17) The life-and-death importance of helping each other stay clean, sober, and alive makes our outward differences trivial. Still, if this is causing you problems, this assignment may give you some valuable ways to overcome the challenge and make the most of your recovery program.

1. Have you read any of the stories in the back sections of the Big Books used by different 12-step programs? Some of the authors are members of minorities among their recovery groups, and they have wrestled with issues of feeling different, conspicuous, and not fitting in. Here are some stories to look for:

   a. In *Alcoholics Anonymous*, 4th edition, the stories titled "Jim's Story," "He Lived Only to Drink," "Listening to the Wind," "Building a New Life," "A Vision of Recovery," "Grounded," and "Another Chance" relate the experiences of people belonging to different minority groups who found ways to feel at home and use the tools of that program to stay sober.

   b. In the book *Narcotics Anonymous*, read the story titled "An Indian without a Tribe."

2. Choose either or both of these books and read the stories mentioned. What do you have in common with the authors of the stories you read?

   _____

   _____

   _____

   _____

3. In addition to the stories in the books, other recovery program literature may help you. Check with your meeting's literature representative, your program's nearest central office, and any web sites that may feature your program's literature, and get copies of any pamphlets that address special issues or questions of members of your cultural group in recovery. Were you able to find any? _____ If so, were they helpful, and what information was useful to you?

   _____

   _____

   _____

   _____

4. Many others in recovery have had to find solutions to the same problems. One way to find out what has worked for them is to ask them directly. Find a person you identify with in your recovery program who strikes you as having the quality of sobriety and recovery you would like to have, and ask that person how he or she dealt with any problems of not fitting in because of looking or sounding different. After doing this, what useful feedback did this person give you?

   _____

   _____

   _____

   _____

5. Finally, your program may have some meetings in your area that are formally or informally made up mostly or entirely of members

of your culture. Use a meeting schedule, contact your nearest central office, and ask around to find out when and where any of these groups meet (*note:* If there aren't any, maybe it would be a good idea to talk with some people experienced in sobriety about starting a group). Once you've located a meeting or meetings, see whether you feel more comfortable there than at other meetings. How was your experience different from your experiences in other recovery settings?

_____

_____

_____

_____

Be sure to bring this handout to your next session with your therapist and talk about your thoughts and feelings about the exercise.

# 12-STEP RECOVERY ISSUES
# IN JAIL OR PRISON

## GOALS OF THIS EXERCISE

1. Enable greater identification and affiliation with others participating in 12-step programs.

2. Identify and use 12-step program literature and resources relevant to the needs of recovering, incarcerated clients.

3. Increase step-focused interactions with peers and other 12-step program members.

## SUGGESTIONS FOR PROCESSING THIS
## EXERCISE WITH CLIENTS

This exercise is designed for inmate clients in early recovery. Clinicians may have to adapt this activity to the limits placed on clients' actions by particular correctional institutions in which they are incarcerated. Greater time should be allowed for this assignment than for others because it requires more reading and discussion and may require clients to obtain literature they do not have access to. Follow-up should include asking the client about progress or problems with this assignment at each contact before the assignment is due and a review by the therapist of the literature the client is reading and of any correspondence with recovering people outside the correctional institution via a "Loners," "Bridging the Gap," or other prison outreach program. Once the initial part of the assignment is done, the therapist should continue to periodically raise the topic of working together with other inmates in recovery and encourage the client to make this part of his or her recovery program.

# 12-STEP RECOVERY ISSUES IN JAIL OR PRISON

Trying to get clean and sober or maintain your sobriety while incarcerated can be especially hard. The environment around you may be one where alcohol or other drugs are even easier to get than on the outside, and you are probably facing greater stress and temptation to drink, use, or otherwise engage in addictive behavior. Still, many successfully recovering people began their new lives while they were in jail or prison and have told how they did it.

1. Have you read any of the stories in the back sections of the Big Books used by different 12-step programs? Many of the authors have had some experiences in jails or prisons, too many to list here. But for a few this has been a significant part of their recoveries, and they've written about this aspect of their lives in their testimonies. Their stories may be useful for you. Here are some of these stories:

   a. In *Alcoholics Anonymous,* 4th edition, the stories titled "Safe Haven," "Grounded," and "Another Chance" relate the experiences of people whose incarceration is or was a significant part of their recovery.

   b. In the book *Narcotics Anonymous*, try reading the stories titled "A Gift Called Life" and "Jails, Institutions, and Recovery."

   c. *Hope, Faith, and Courage: Stories from the Fellowship of Cocaine Anonymous* includes useful stories titled "True Freedom," "The Great Pretender," and "He Quit Failing."

2. Choose the book related to your recovery program and either or both of the other books if you like and read the stories mentioned.

What do you have in common with the authors of the stories you read?

_____

_____

_____

_____

3. In addition to the stories in the books, other recovery program literature may help you. Check with your meeting's literature representative and if possible your program's nearest central office. If you're able to, get copies of any pamphlets that address special issues or questions of incarcerated people in recovery. Were you able to get any? _____ If so, were they helpful, and what information was useful to you?

_____

_____

_____

_____

4. Many other people in jail or prison are in recovery, and they've had to find solutions to the same problems you face. One way to find out what has worked for them is to ask them directly. Find a person you identify with in your recovery program who strikes you as having the quality of sobriety and recovery you would like to have and ask that person how he or she dealt with any special challenges to staying clean and sober because of being incarcerated. After doing this, what useful feedback did this person give you?

_____

_____

_____

_____

5. Last but not least, your program may have an outreach program for "loners," people who are physically unable to get to many meetings, and there may even be a specific program such as "Bridge the Gap" through which recovering people on the outside can exchange

letters with inmates. Is there a program like this available to you?
_____ If so, part of this assignment is to sign up and start exchanging letters with someone in recovery on the outside. Once you've started doing this, use this space to write about any ways this is helping you stay clean and sober.

_____

_____

_____

_____

Be sure to bring this handout to your next session with your therapist and talk about your thoughts and feelings about the exercise.

# 12-STEP RECOVERY ISSUES FOR PEOPLE WITH CO-OCCURRING MENTAL/EMOTIONAL AND/OR PHYSICAL ILLNESSES

## GOALS OF THIS EXERCISE

1. Enable greater identification and affiliation with others participating in 12-step programs.

2. Increase the understanding of linkages between substance abuse and symptoms of mental and emotional illness.

3. Increase the understanding of 12-step program policies supportive of compliance with psychiatric and psychotherapeutic treatment.

4. Identify and use 12-step program literature and resources relevant to the needs of dually diagnosed recovering people.

5. Increase step-focused interactions with peers and other 12-step program members.

## SUGGESTIONS FOR PROCESSING THIS EXERCISE WITH CLIENTS

This exercise is designed for dually diagnosed clients in early recovery. Greater time should be allowed for this assignment than for others because it requires more reading and discussion and may require clients to obtain literature they do not have access to. Follow-up should include asking the client about progress or problems with this assignment at each contact before the assignment is due and a review by the therapist of the literature the client is reading and of any participation in "Double Trouble" or other 12-step groups or programs specifically for people with dual diagnoses. Once the initial part of the assignment is done, the therapist should continue to periodically raise the topic of working together with other dually diagnosed recovering people and encourage the client to make this part of his or her recovery program.

# 12-STEP RECOVERY ISSUES FOR PEOPLE WITH CO-OCCURRING MENTAL/EMOTIONAL AND/OR PHYSICAL ILLNESSES

If you are one of the many people in recovery who are dually diagnosed, meaning that you have not only an addiction but also a serious mental, emotional, or physical illness or disability, you face a greater challenge than someone who has only the addiction or only the other issue. Most people struggling with addiction also experience some depression, anxiety, or other mental distress, and many also suffer some physical consequences of their addictive lifestyles. However, this assignment is for you if your coexisting problem is serious enough to be a crisis in your life in its own right.

Although you face a tough set of challenges, you also have a lot of company. Many others have overcome similar problems. One of the first lines in the section of the book *Alcoholics Anonymous* titled "How It Works," which is read at the beginning of many meetings, states: "There are those, too, with grave mental and emotional disorders, but many of them do recover if they have the capacity to be honest." (Alcoholics Anonymous, p. 58) There is great support available within the rooms of the 12-step programs, as well as through psychotherapy and other sources.

1. People who engage in addictive behaviors, especially involving alcohol or other drugs, are more likely than others to suffer from psychiatric or other medical illness, and people with mental and emotional disorders or chronic medical problems are at higher than average risk to have problems with addictions. Some people develop medical or psychiatric problems as a result of their addictive lifestyles, particularly with psychedelic drugs or with prolonged heavy use of stimulants such as methamphetamine. Please describe

any ways you feel your addictive lifestyle has led to your becoming
seriously ill in other ways:

_____

_____

_____

_____

2. Sometimes the connection between addiction and other serious illness works in the other direction. The mental, emotional, or other
serious illnesses come first; and when people use addictive substances or behaviors (alcohol, other drugs, eating, overwork, or any
other addiction) to try to control or cope with the original problems,
they become dependent on those substances or behaviors. Please
describe how your coexisting problem's symptoms may have led
you to drink, use, or otherwise behave addictively in the search for
relief of those symptoms:

_____

_____

_____

_____

3. If you know someone in your 12-step group who is succeeding in
overcoming both addiction and another serious illness, how are
they doing this? Could you use some of their methods? If so, what
are they doing that you can also do?

_____

_____

_____

_____

4. Some techniques people use to cope with psychiatric or medical
problems, such as the use of antipsychotic drugs and other prescribed mind-altering or pain-relieving medications, may seem not
to fit into 12-step recovery from addiction. If you are under a doctor's instructions to take medications for another problem, have you
talked about your addictive issues with the doctor who prescribed

the medications? _____ What did the doctor tell you about this?

_____

_____

_____

_____

5.  Are you aware of the policies that AA and other 12-step programs have developed about the use of prescribed medications? What have others told you, and what do you believe those programs have to say about this?

_____

_____

_____

_____

6.  If you are under a doctor's care and taking prescribed medications, what would be the consequences if you stopped taking those medications?

_____

_____

_____

_____

7.  The position of AA and other 12-step programs is that if you are being treated by a doctor who understands addiction, and you have explained to that doctor that you are in recovery and don't want to relapse, you should then take whatever medications your doctor prescribes, exactly as instructed. If you do this you are not giving up your sobriety, and for some people, such as those who need antidepressants, this may be the only way to stay alive and in recovery. The Alcoholics Anonymous General Service Office publishes a pamphlet on this topic titled "The AA Member— Medications and Other Drugs." It offers guidelines including saying

No AA Member Plays Doctor. Playing doctor means either deciding to take prescription medications without a doctor's prescription or in any way other than a doctor instructs us to do, or giving other people advice about their medications.

Do you know others in a 12-step program who take prescribed mind-altering medications? How do they avoid falling into the trap of substance abuse?

_____

_____

_____

_____

8. Have you read any of the stories in the back sections of the Big Books used by different 12-step programs? A number of these authors have also suffered from other serious mental, emotional, or physical illnesses. Here are some stories to look for, with the co-existing problems the authors have faced:

   a. In *Alcoholics Anonymous,* 4th edition, in the entries titled "The Man Who Mastered Fear" (agoraphobia), "The Missing Link" (depression), "Winner Takes All" (complete blindness), "Twice Gifted" (cirrhosis of the liver), "On the Move" (multiple sclerosis), and "Freedom from Bondage" (depression/anxiety disorders), alcoholics who have also suffered from other debilitating illnesses, either psychiatric or medical, tell how they not only stayed sober but often found ways to use the tools of AA to cope with their other disorders.

   b. In the book *Narcotics Anonymous*, read the stories titled "Why Me? Why Not Me?" (multiple medical issues) and "Fearful Mother" (diabetes).

   c. *Hope, Faith, and Courage: Stories from the Fellowship of Cocaine Anonymous* includes the story titled "Living for the Moment" (HIV).

   d. In *Overeaters Anonymous*, read "Sink the Lollipop" (kidney disease).

e. *Emotions Anonymous* has the story entitled "Life Has Just Begun" (cancer).

f. In *Co-Dependents Anonymous*, you may identify with parts of "My Thanksgiving Story" (diabetes, ulcers, colitis, blindness).

9. Choose the book related to your recovery program and some other books if you like and read the stories mentioned. What do you have in common with the authors of the stories you read?

_____

_____

_____

10. In addition to the stories in the books, other recovery program literature may help. Check with your meeting's literature representative, your program's nearest central office, and any web sites that may feature your program's literature, and get copies of any pamphlets that address special issues or questions of dually diagnosed people in recovery. Were you able to find any? _____
If so, were they helpful, and what information was useful to you?

_____

_____

_____

11. Many other dually diagnosed people in recovery have had to find solutions to the same problems. One way to find out what has worked for them is to ask them directly. Find a person you identify with in your recovery program who strikes you as having the quality of sobriety and recovery you would like to have, and ask that person how he or she dealt with any problems of not fitting in because of problems above and beyond his or her addiction. After doing this, what useful feedback did this person give you?

_____

_____

_____

12. Finally, your program may have some dual diagnosis meetings in your area. These often go by names such as "Double Trouble." Contact your nearest central office to find out when and where any of these groups meet (*note:* If there aren't any, it might be a good idea to talk with some other dually diagnosed people experienced in sobriety about starting a group). Once you find a meeting or meetings, see whether you feel more comfortable there than at other meetings. How was it different from other recovery settings?

_____

_____

_____

_____

Be sure to bring this handout to your next session with your therapist and talk about your thoughts and feelings about the exercise.

# UNDERSTANDING 12-STEP RECOVERY FOR LOVED ONES OF PEOPLE WITH ADDICTIONS

## GOALS OF THIS EXERCISE

1. Enable greater understanding of the nature of addiction, including nonchemical addictions.

2. Gain familiarity with the workings of 12-step programs and the resources they offer to addicted loved ones.

3. Identify and use 12-step programs, literature, and resources available for family members and friends of people with addictions.

## SUGGESTIONS FOR PROCESSING THIS EXERCISE WITH CLIENTS

This exercise is designed for clients who are family members, close friends, and other people who are in emotionally significant relationships with addicted people in early recovery. Greater time should be allowed for this assignment than for others because it requires more reading and discussion and may require clients to obtain literature they do not have access to. Follow-up should include asking the client about progress or problems with this assignment at each contact before the assignment is due and a review by the therapist of the literature the client is reading and of any attendance at, or participation in, either open 12-step meetings for the addiction suffered by another or meetings of Al-Anon, Nar-Anon, Co-Dependents Anonymous, Gam-Anon, or other programs for people in situations like the client's. Once the initial part of the assignment is done, the therapist should continue to periodically raise the topic of working together with other people in important relationships with addicts and encourage the client to make this part of his or her recovery program.

# UNDERSTANDING 12-STEP RECOVERY FOR LOVED ONES OF PEOPLE WITH ADDICTIONS

If you are a spouse, partner, parent, child, sibling, other relative, or close friend of someone with an addiction, you have probably experienced many painful, complicated, and confusing feelings. It may be hard to understand how someone who says he or she cares deeply about you can be inconsiderate, dishonest, undependable, and sometimes cruel. When you are told that this is a disease and that terrible behavior is a symptom of the disease, it may sound like an excuse rather than an explanation.

Or, if your experience is like others, you may understand and believe that the addiction really is an illness rather than a sign of bad character or lack of caring, but you may feel helplessness and despair when you try to figure out how you can help the person you love.

If you are doing this assignment, you are probably in counseling either together with the addicted person or on your own. This exercise has two purposes: first, to help you understand how the disease of addiction works, and second, to help you find ways to both help this person, if you wish, and at the same time take care of yourself.

1. After decades of skepticism, the American Medical Association (AMA) defined alcoholism as a disease in the 1950s. The American Psychiatric Association (APA) has defined any form of substance abuse or dependence as a form of mental illness and therefore a disease.

    The book *Alcoholics Anonymous,* the text of that program often called the Big Book states: "An illness of this sort—and we have come to believe it an illness—involves those about us in a way no other human sickness can. If a person has cancer all are sorry for him and no one is angry or hurt. But not so with the alcoholic illness, for with it there goes annihilation of all the things worth while in life. It engulfs all whose lives touch the sufferer's. It brings misunderstanding, fierce resentment, financial insecurity, disgusted friends and employers, warped lives of blameless children, sad wives and parents—anyone can increase the list" (p. 18). When you think about the AMA and APA calling this an illness and read this paragraph, what are your first thoughts and feelings in reaction? Is this easy for you to believe, or do you find it hard to agree with?

_____

_____

_____

_____

2. It may help to think about the reasons these medical organizations have defined dependence on alcohol or any other chemical as a disease. Their reasoning is based on three factors: chemical dependence has clear-cut symptoms (these vary depending on the chemical involved), it has a clear progression that it follows if not effectively treated, and it can be treated. Do you agree that addiction fits this description? _____ Take a moment and think of several other conditions that fit those same conditions, anything from heart disease to chicken pox. Can you think of one that you would not call an illness? If so, what is it? _____

3. It may also help to do some research on your own. As the next part of this assignment, get in contact with Alcoholics Anonymous or another 12-step program such as Narcotics Anonymous or Cocaine Anonymous in your community. If possible, find the program dealing with the specific type of addiction affecting the person to whom you are close. Find out when you can go to some *open meetings*. These are meetings where you don't have to have that particular problem to attend. People who are just curious are welcome. Go to at least three meetings. At the meetings you will probably be asked to introduce yourself by first name only. You can give your first name and, if you wish, add that you are concerned about someone you know and want to learn more about their problem. During the meeting, listen for people describing situations similar to any you may have experienced and pay attention to their

thoughts and feelings about those situations. Pay special attention to those who have been clean and sober a few years or longer, as they are likely to have more insight. After attending three meetings, use this space to record whatever you have learned about addiction as an illness:

_____

_____

_____

_____

4. This may make sense when it comes to addiction to a chemical like alcohol or cocaine. However, you may be dealing with someone whose addiction is nonphysical. This could be compulsive eating, workaholism, compulsive spending, gambling addiction, sex addiction, or another behavioral problem that doesn't involve using a drug but causes the same kind of chaos otherwise. It can be a lot harder to see how these things can also be addictions.

   The key is to recognize that addiction means being hooked on something that makes a person feel better very quickly, either by increasing pleasure or by relieving physical or emotional pain, but causes more problems than it's worth in the long term. All the activities listed previously are activities people engage in to feel better, and they work in the short term, but cause greater pain in the long term. Does this make sense to you? _____ If not, please talk about it with your therapist.

5. For the second purpose of this lesson, learning to cope with the addictive behavior while taking care of yourself, it's useful to draw on the experiences of others. The challenge here is often figuring out how to let addicted people be accountable for their own actions without trying to rescue them, without trying to fix them and make them get better. Have you tried rescuing and fixing your addict? _____ Did it cause the addictive behavior to improve? _____ If there is another way to handle this that has been proven to work, are you willing to learn more and try it? _____

6. The next step is to try attending some 12-step meetings that are not for the people with the addiction but rather are for people in your

situation. They use the same 12 steps as the various Anonymous programs, except that instead of acknowledging that they are powerless over their own drug or habit, they admit they are unable to control the other person's problem. For people close to alcoholics, the best organization to try is Al-Anon; for those involved with people with other addictions, it may be Nar-Anon, for family and friends of drug addicts, Gam-Anon, for those involved with gambling addicts, or another organization. A program that is useful for all is Co-Dependents Anonymous (CoDA). Codependency can be defined as worrying so much about someone else's life that we neglect our own. Are there meetings of Al-Anon, Nar-Anon, Gam-Anon, or CoDA in your area? _____ If so, the final part of this assignment is to attend at least six meetings to watch, listen, and learn. See whether you identify with the people you see and hear, and see whether they are finding solutions to the same problems you face. After you've gone to six meetings, use this space to record your thoughts:

_____

_____

_____

_____

Be sure to bring this handout to your next session with your therapist and talk about your thoughts and feelings about the exercise.

**Section III**

# LESSON PLANS

Section III contains eight psychoeducational lesson plans related to 12-step work. These lesson plans use visual, auditory, and tactile/kinesthetic learning styles: The information can be presented in either slideshow or handout format, accompanied by lecture and discussion, while the group members write their notes. These group lessons complement the individual homework assignments in Section II. Rather than duplicating the content of the homework assignments, the lesson plans use a group format to give clients concrete guidance in applying the principles of 12-step recovery in several areas of daily life that are frequent sources of stress and may become relapse triggers unless clients gain coping skills to handle them.

The recommended method for use of the lesson plans is a combination of lecture and interactive discussion. Each lesson plan offers questions to start an initial discussion among group members, inviting them to share their own experiences and perceptions related to the topic. As the presenter proceeds through the lesson plan, it is recommended that the group be invited to discuss their related thoughts and experiences after each subtopic is presented.

In addition to the lesson plans, the CD-ROM accompanying this book includes Microsoft PowerPoint presentations that can be used in two ways. With a computer connected to an LCD projector or by printing the files on transparencies, the PowerPoint presentations can be used as slide shows to accompany the lesson plan lectures and discussions. The PowerPoint slides can also be printed and used as handouts to complement presentation of the material in the lesson plans, providing group members with a structured way to take notes.

# WHAT TO EXPECT IN A 12-STEP GROUP

**DURATION:** 2 hours 0 minutes

**TARGET POPULATION:** Clients in treatment or early recovery from addictive disorders

**FACILITY REQUIRED:** Classroom with desks or chairs and tables

**MATERIAL AND EQUIPMENT REQUIRED:**

Flip chart pads and stand, white board, or chalkboard

Markers or chalk

Optional: Computer with LCD projector or overhead projector and screen

Handouts

**PERFORMANCE OBJECTIVES:** On completion of this presentation the participant will be able to:

1.  Demonstrate knowledge of typical activities in 12-step groups and meetings.

2.  Demonstrate the ability to integrate 12-step activities into personal-recovery and relapse-prevention planning.

3.  Demonstrate practical application of the use of 12-step group activities to enhance recovery and abstinence from addiction.

**METHODS/TECHNIQUES OF INSTRUCTION:** Lecture and discussion

## I. INTRODUCTION:

**A. The subject and why it is important:** Ask group members to brainstorm about why they believe it might be important to know about what happens in 12-step groups. Engage the group in a brief discussion of ways they think that their lives might be better because of participation in 12-step programs. Finally, ask the group what they would expect a 12-step group to be like, based on what they know. For each question, write the group's answers on a board, flipchart, or transparency, using check marks to show duplicate answers.

**B. Group policy (learning goals, policy on questions):** Explain to group members that they are expected to achieve the following learning goals:

    1. *Learning goals:*

        (a) On completion of this presentation, group members will demonstrate knowledge of typical activities in 12-step groups and meetings.

        (b) On completion of this presentation, group members will demonstrate the ability to integrate 12-step activities into personal-recovery and relapse-prevention planning.

        (c) On completion of this presentation, group members will demonstrate the practical application of 12-step group activities to enhance recovery and abstinence from addiction.

    2. *Questions:* The instructor may either have group members hold their questions until the end of the presentation or ask questions spontaneously. If participation is a high priority, we recommend spontaneous questions; if brevity is more important, it works better to hold questions until the end.

II. **12-STEP MEETINGS: Present the following to the group and invite questions and discussion:**

A. **12-step meetings in general:** Most 12-step meetings are similar in structure.

1. *Leadership:* A member of the group chairs the meeting. The group may choose someone to chair a given meeting on a long-term basis, or someone may volunteer at random when the meeting is about to begin. Some groups have rules that a member must have been in recovery for a minimum amount of time, such as six months, before he or she is allowed to chair meetings. The chairperson is responsible for starting and ending the meeting on time, for ensuring the meeting format is followed, and for maintaining order during the meeting.

2. *Opening:* In most meetings the chairperson introduces himself or herself, then asks the group to join in a moment of silence followed by a prayer, usually the Serenity Prayer *(God grant me the serenity to accept the things I cannot change, the courage to change the things I can, and the wisdom to know the difference).* Participation in the prayer is not required. Following the opening prayer, the chairperson may ask new members and visitors present to introduce themselves by first names. People normally respond by giving their names and identifying themselves as having the problem that the group exists to address ("My name is _____ and I'm an alcoholic/addict/gambling addict/etc."). The chairperson may read announcements of upcoming events or group policies. The chairperson usually asks members of the group to read selections from program literature including the 12 steps and often the 12 traditions as they apply to that group. Depending on the format of the meeting, the chairperson may then choose a topic, ask another member to choose a topic, or introduce a speaker.

3. *Main portion of the meeting:* Depending on the meeting's format, most of the time may be used for

discussion of a chosen topic, listening to a speaker, or reading and discussion of a portion of a book related to the program.

4. *Tradition 7:* Sometime during the meeting the chairperson reminds members that according to Tradition 7 every group must be self-supporting and then passes a collection basket. All are free to put money in the basket but no contribution is required or expected.

5. *Closing:* A few minutes before the meeting is scheduled to end, the chairperson may ask whether anyone present has a "burning desire" to say something. The chairperson may also make an announcement reminding members of the obligation to protect one another's anonymity and may have a member read a short closing passage from program literature. Meetings are most often concluded by having members form a circle while holding hands and join in a closing prayer such as the Serenity Prayer, the Lord's Prayer, or another chosen by the group or the chairperson. As with the opening prayer, all are free to join in the prayer, to silently say a different prayer of their own choice, or to decline to join in prayer at all.

6. *Variations:* Every group is different, and may add or eliminate parts of the sequence described here. Some common variations include the use of different prayers including those of non-Christian faith communities, dedication of portions of the meeting time to silent meditation, and presentation of anniversary chips to members celebrating sobriety anniversaries.

B. **Types of meetings:** There are several types of meetings in all 12-step programs.

1. *Open/closed:* Meetings may be designated as open—anyone can attend—or closed—only people who are trying to overcome the addictive problem that program exists to address may attend. In an open meeting, the chairperson may ask that anyone present who does not

suffer from that group's subject addiction listen but not share in the discussion.

2. *Discussion:* In a discussion meeting, the chairperson chooses a topic related to addiction and recovery or asks another member to choose the topic, and group members then share their own experiences and thoughts on the topic. The chairperson may choose group members to share in several ways. He or she may call on members, start with one person and proceed around the room in order by where members are sitting, designate the meeting a *tag meeting* in which each member who shares chooses the next member, or designate it an open meeting in which anyone who feels the urge to share may do so.

3. *Book study:* A book study meeting is dedicated to collective reading and discussion of a book chosen from the official literature of the program. Usually, a member will read a short passage, such as a paragraph, and briefly discuss it. Another member then reads the next passage and discusses that and so on throughout the time available.

4. *Birthday:* Many groups have a monthly birthday meeting at which anniversary chips are given to members celebrating sobriety anniversaries that month. Usually, each person who gets a chip is invited to speak briefly. These meetings often include the serving of birthday cakes.

5. *Group conscience:* Most groups hold a business meeting called a *group conscience* monthly or quarterly. At this meeting, the group hears reports from its treasurer and other officers and votes on decisions, such as whether to host special events, whether to add or change group policies and rules, and what to do about any problems that may arise in the group.

6. *Special population:* Some groups are organized specifically by and for special groups within the membership

of the program. These can include meetings for women only, men only, young people's meetings, gay and lesbian meetings, meetings for members of a particular faith group, or others. A special meeting may or may not allow people who are not part of that group to attend.

7. *Nonsmoking or smoking:* Many meetings are non-smoking meetings.

C. **Good manners in meetings:** Here are some basic guidelines to follow in attending 12-step meetings.

1. *Respect the group's rules and policies:* Don't smoke in a nonsmoking meeting. If the group has a policy that members avoid profanity, don't swear while sharing. In general, respect the customs of the group as explained in the announcements read by the chairperson.

2. *Stick to the topic:* People sharing at meetings should generally try to stay focused on the topic chosen for that meeting and talk about their problems with the addiction that are that program's focus.

3. *Keep it brief:* Except for the speaker at a speaker meeting, a member who is sharing should avoid taking up too much of the group's time so that as many people as possible will have the chance to talk.

4. *Don't be disruptive:* Avoid side conversations, talking on cell phones, walking in late, coming and going during meetings, interrupting people, allowing children to be noisy or run around, or other practices that are distracting and make it harder for others to hear and concentrate on the meeting.

III. **OTHER KEY ELEMENTS IN 12-STEP PROGRAMS: Present the following to the group and invite questions and discussion:**

A. **Step work:** This may seem so obvious it doesn't need to be pointed out, but many people do try to stay clean and sober only by attending meetings and not by also working the steps. It's very important to work through the steps with a sponsor.

B. **Sponsorship:** Most members of 12-step programs have sponsors. A sponsor is a mentor, an experienced member of the program who guides the recovering person in working the 12 steps and in coping with challenges to his or her recovery. In choosing a sponsor, it is best to avoid selecting anyone with whom you already have a close relationship or with whom there is the risk of a romantic attraction developing. For that reason, most people avoid choosing sponsors of the opposite gender and family members to sponsor them. Every person differs in his or her approach to being a sponsor or working with a sponsor, but some common practices are attending meetings together, frequently meeting individually, and having the sponsor guide the sponsee through the process of working the steps in a structured way.

C. **Service work:** Doing work that helps other addicts and the program is a vital and necessary part of every recovery program. Service work can take many forms. Some common ones are:

1. *Making 12th-Step calls:* This refers to accompanying other members of the program when calling or visiting people who have contacted the program and asked for information or help in overcoming their own addictions.

2. *Sponsorship:* As was previously described, service work includes sponsoring another recovering person.

3. *"Trusted servant" positions:* Service work includes participation as one of the elected officers of a group, such as the treasurer, or one who is designated to be the liaison to other meetings or to the central office or the district.

4. *Meeting support:* Much service work consists of setting up meeting rooms, making coffee, cleaning up

afterward, and general housekeeping work in meeting places.

5. *Central office work:* Many programs, especially larger programs such as Alcoholics Anonymous (AA), Narcotics Anonymous (NA), and Al-Anon, staff central offices in larger communities. They need volunteers to answer phones, provide information, and send members on 12th-Step calls to help people who call with a need for information or assistance.

**D. Fellowship:** Another key part of participating in a 12-step program is joining in the social activity in the group. This can be the most enjoyable part and may include going to coffee with other members of the group after meetings, participating in dances and picnics, helping to organize holiday events, and other less formal social activities.

## IV. WHAT NOT TO EXPECT: Present the following to the group and invite questions and discussion:

**A. 12-step programs are not religious:** There is a lot of talk about God in the literature and meetings of 12-step programs. However, the program of the 12 steps is spiritual rather than religious. No 12-step program is connected with any religious denomination. One of the most important principles is that every member has not only the right but also the need to find his or her own understanding of a Higher Power (what that person may think of as God or in whatever way he or she chooses). Although meetings usually open and close with prayers, many members choose not to participate in the prayers and either substitute other prayers with which they're more comfortable, find other ways to silently commune with whatever Higher Power they've found, or simply meditate in silence for a few moments.

**B. There are no membership requirements or dues:** Every 12-step program is free and open to anyone who wants to participate. As Tradition 3 says, the only requirement for membership is a desire to stop living the addictive lifestyle.

C. **No one is in charge:** There are no officials in any 12-step group with the power to tell other members what or what not to do. Most groups do have secretaries, treasurers, and other officers, but these members are called trusted servants and take their instructions from the group rather than being in charge of the group.

## V. CONCLUSION:

A. **Summary:** This presentation briefly covered the events in 12-step meetings, several types of meetings, how to behave in meetings, and other key elements of 12-step programs. This information is important because knowing what to expect makes it easier to get the most benefit from participating in a 12-step program, and more people who succeed in staying clean and sober do so by participating in 12-step programs than any other way.

B. **Review the learning goals:**

1. Demonstrate knowledge of typical activities in 12-step groups and meetings.

2. Demonstrate the ability to integrate 12-step activities into personal-recovery and relapse-prevention planning.

3. Demonstrate the practical application of 12-step group activities to enhance recovery and abstinence from addiction.

C. **Questions/Discussion**

# 12-STEP MEETING REVIEW AND ANALYSIS

**DURATION:** 1 hour 30 minutes

**TARGET POPULATION:** Clients in treatment or early recovery from addictive disorders

**FACILITY REQUIRED:** Classroom with desks or chairs and tables

**MATERIAL AND EQUIPMENT REQUIRED:**

Flip chart pads and stand, white board, or chalkboard

Markers or chalk

Optional: Computer with LCD projector or overhead projector and screen

Handouts

**PERFORMANCE OBJECTIVES:** On completion of this presentation the participant will be able to:

1. Demonstrate knowledge of important elements in 12-step meetings.

2. Demonstrate the ability to integrate information and concepts gained in 12-step meetings into personal-recovery and relapse-prevention planning.

3. Demonstrate practical application of use of 12-step meeting review and analysis to maximize benefits of participation.

**METHODS/TECHNIQUES OF INSTRUCTION:** Lecture and discussion

## I. INTRODUCTION:

A. **The subject and why it is important:** Ask group members to brainstorm why they believe it might be important to know about what happens in 12-step groups. Engage the group in a brief discussion of ways they think that their lives might be better because of participation in 12-step programs. Finally, ask the group what they would expect a 12-step group to be like, based on what they know. For each question, write the groups' answers on a board, flip chart, or transparency, using check marks to show duplicate answers.

B. **Group policy (learning goals, policy on questions):** Explain to group members that they are expected to achieve the following learning goals:

1. *Learning goals:*

   (a) On completion of this presentation, group members will demonstrate knowledge of important elements in 12-step meetings.

   (b) On completion of this presentation, group members will demonstrate the ability to integrate information and concepts gained in 12-step meetings into personal-recovery and relapse-prevention planning.

   (c) On completion of this presentation, group members will demonstrate the practical application of the 12-step meeting review and analysis to maximize the benefits of participation.

2. *Questions:* The instructor may either have group members hold their questions until the end of the presentation or ask questions spontaneously. If participation is a high priority, we recommend spontaneous

questions; if brevity is more important, it works better to hold questions until the end.

II. **12-STEP MEETING REVIEW: As preparation, have group members attend a 12-step meeting together, then individually complete Exercise II-E, the 12-Step Meeting Review/Critique Form. Lead the group in going through the questions on the homework handout, comparing their answers and discussing differences in their perceptions. Focus the group primarily on the following questions and topics:**

A. **Main topic of the meeting:** Guide the group in examining any differences in their perceptions and interpretations of the topic and the possible reasons they might have interpreted it differently, based on their own concerns and life experiences.

B. **Thoughts and feelings in response to the topic and sharing:** Again, guide the group in examining differences in their perceptions and evaluations, both fundamental differences, such as whether their feelings were positive or negative, and more subtle differences, such as how their feelings related to their particular interpretations of the topic. Guide the group in reflecting on common themes and variations in their responses and reasons they might have shared in some responses and differed in others.

C. **Identifying with others' sharing in the meeting:** Guide the group in considering why each person may have been able or unable to relate to others and their experiences. Look for common elements, especially those shared by group members with different backgrounds (differences in gender, age, socioeconomic status, etc.).

D. **Other thoughts and feelings:** Prompt the group in sharing and examining thoughts and feelings about other issues and about their own life situations that were inspired by things they heard shared. Again, focus on common elements reported by group members and the reasons they might have shared those reactions, then consider differences in the same way.

E. **What group members felt they gained:** Poll the group on what each member felt he or she gained from the meeting and invite them to give each other feedback.

F. **Reexamination:** Ask group members to review their own responses again and ask what they would add or change based on the discussion immediately preceding.

G. **Effective use of meeting critique and analysis:** Guide the members of the group in examining any benefit they feel was gained from the process of analysis and discussion just completed, then lead them to consider ways in which they could adapt this technique to use in settings outside this presentation. In particular, lead them in considering how they could use this method in working with 12-step sponsors and in working on particularly troublesome issues.

## III. CONCLUSION:

A. **Summary:** This presentation briefly covered the results and benefits of reviewing and analyzing 12-step meetings. This information is important because knowing how to get the most benefit from participating in 12-step meetings is important to maximizing the likelihood of staying clean and sober.

B. **Review the learning goals:**

1. Demonstrate knowledge of important elements in 12-step meetings.

2. Demonstrate the ability to integrate information and concepts gained in 12-step meetings into personal-recovery and relapse-prevention planning.

3. Demonstrate practical application of use of 12-step meeting review and analysis to maximize benefits of participation.

## C. Questions/Discussion

# PROBLEMS AND SOLUTIONS IN EARLY 12-STEP RECOVERY

**DURATION:** 3 hours 0 minutes

**TARGET POPULATION:** Clients in treatment or early recovery from addictive disorders

**FACILITY REQUIRED:** Classroom with desks or chairs and tables

**MATERIAL AND EQUIPMENT REQUIRED:**

Flip chart pads and stand, white board, or chalkboard

Markers or chalk

Optional: Computer with LCD projector or overhead projector and screen

Handouts

**PERFORMANCE OBJECTIVES:** On completion of this presentation the participant will be able to:

1. Demonstrate knowledge of at least four common problems in early 12-step recovery.

2. Demonstrate understanding of at least one effective coping strategy for each of the problems listed for the first performance objective.

3. Describe personal plans for practical application of solutions to common problems in early 12-step recovery.

**METHODS/TECHNIQUES OF INSTRUCTION:** Lecture and discussion

## I. INTRODUCTION:

A. **The subject and why it is important:** Ask group members to identify the biggest problems they are experiencing in connection with recovery, other than just staying free of drinking, drug use, or other primary addictive behaviors. Write their answers on a board, flipchart, or transparency, using check marks to show duplicate answers. Ask the group how each problem could affect a newly recovering person's abstinence from substance use or other addictive/compulsive behaviors. Ask whether any of the problems identified can be solved by abstinence from substance use without other changes in lifestyle. Tell the group that the information in this presentation is based on the experiences of many others who have been in the position that they are in now and is given to increase the group members' chances of success and help them achieve the best quality of life.

B. **Group policy (learning goals, policy on questions):** Explain to group members and advise them that they will be evaluated to check accomplishment of these goals.

1. *Learning goals:*

   (a) On completion of this presentation, group members will demonstrate knowledge of at least four common problems in early 12-step recovery.

   (b) On completion of this presentation, group members will demonstrate an understanding of at least one effective coping strategy for each of the problems listed for the first performance objective.

   (c) On completion of this presentation, group members will describe personal plans for practical application of solutions to common problems in early 12-step recovery.

2. *Questions:* The instructor may either have group members hold their questions until the end of the presentation or ask questions spontaneously. If participation is a high priority, we recommend spontaneous questions; if brevity is more important, it works better to hold questions until the end.

## II. COMMON PROBLEMS AND ISSUES IN EARLY RECOVERY:

A. **Dislike of meetings:** This may be a common complaint for people in treatment programs that require group members to attend AA, NA, or other 12-step recovery program meetings. Many people find they initially dislike 12-step meetings and attend only because they are required to do so but later find that they come to value the meetings and want to continue. This process often takes weeks or months. The following are methods used by many to make meetings more enjoyable:

1. *Shop around:* Each person should go to as many different groups as possible and find the ones he or she likes best. Try other programs as well as the program dealing with the primary addiction. Every group has its own personality; some will fit while others won't. To succeed, it helps to find people with whom he or she has a lot in common and ask those people which meetings they like best.

2. *Go with friends:* Attending a meeting with friends or family members, then discussing it afterward, makes it a more interesting and enjoyable experience. This is sometimes described as *the meeting after the meeting* that takes place in the car or van on the way home (or back to a treatment center). Going with friends can also help when people are nervous about going to meetings they have not attended before.

3. *Participate by reading, helping out, and speaking up at meetings:* Even if they only bring someone a cup of

coffee or give their names and a brief comment (e.g., mentioning that they could relate to something someone said) most people leave a meeting feeling better than when they say or do nothing to interact with others.

4. *Find a preferred type of meeting:* Some people prefer step-study or book-study meetings, speaker meetings, or open topic/sharing meetings. Each person should try them all and find out which format he or she likes best, then seek out meetings with that format. A person may also find that he or she is most comfortable in a meeting that is small or large, smoking or nonsmoking, open or closed, stag (one sex only) or mixed, oriented toward a certain age range, gay/lesbian, in a language other than English, and so on.

5. *Go a little early, stay a little late:* Most meetings include some socializing before and after, and people are usually friendly but not nosy. This is a good chance to meet people one on one and ask questions a person might not want to share with the whole room, especially in early recovery.

6. *Pick a home group:* A home group is like a second family where regular attendees are known, accepted, expected, and missed if they aren't there. That's a good feeling for most people.

7. *Help start a new meeting:* If any individual is one of a small group that gets in at the beginning of a group's formation, that group's personality will be based partly on that individual's personality and preferences. For a person who is looking for a particular type of meeting or one at a certain time, chances are some other people are too. It is a good idea to have at least a couple of people with a few years of recovery to help launch a new meeting, but a newcomer to recovery can help put his or her own stamp on it.

8. *Give the meetings some time:* For most people, meetings feel strange at first. It's wise for a newcomer to allow some time to get used to the experience. Many who are uncomfortable at first come to look forward to meetings.

B. **Higher Power issues:** Most people have trouble with the idea of surrendering to a Higher Power. It doesn't fit with the beliefs and values of many, it doesn't seem to make sense, and it doesn't fit with the pattern many addicts have of trying to control and manipulate everything and everyone around them. Here are some tactics that have worked for many people:

1. *Read the words "as we understood him" and think about their meaning:* The 12 steps don't ask anyone to believe in a particular version of God, Allah, the Great Spirit, the Force, or whatever. If anyone can believe that there *could* be a power greater than them, that's all they need at the start. People have chosen as their Higher Power any of the following things, or many more:

   (a) Their principles of right and wrong

   (b) Their groups

   (c) Their conscience or "inner voice"

   (d) The God they were raised to believe in

   (e) A mystery they hope to understand later on

   (f) Nature

   (g) Time

2. *Find experienced people at a meeting that the newly recovering person can relate to and ask them their views about the Higher Power:* Since many recovering people struggle with this issue, if the new arrival feels he or she has a lot in common with others, the chances are good that those others have had the same doubts;

and if they found solutions that work for them, those solutions might work for the newcomer too.

3. *Read about it:* There is some good material about this in various places: in the AA Big Book's "Chapter to the Agnostic," other books in sections of bookstores devoted to both religion and addiction and recovery, workbooks, and some pamphlets that are available at some meetings. An especially useful book is *A Skeptic's Guide to the 12 Steps* by Phillip Z., a man who entered a 12-step program as an atheist.

4. *Design a personal God:* A newly recovering addict can think about what he or she was taught about God, then ask alternatively what kind of God would make sense based on his or her experiences and how people might be able to see that God at work in the world. What would the evidence be? Then if the newly sober person is willing to watch for that evidence, he or she may start seeing it.

5. *Bring the subject up at a meeting:* If one person raises the topic and says he or she is having trouble with the concept of a Higher Power, others will respond to say "me, too!" or to share their experience in resolving this dilemma. There's nothing wrong with having doubts and questions; and in a healthy group, they will be respected and accepted, though others may disagree and share their own views hoping each person can find something in them with which to agree.

6. *Talk about it with a sponsor:* If the new person has chosen a sponsor with whom he or she feels comfortable and has much in common, the sponsor may have gone through the same struggle and found a solution the sponsee can use.

Note to presenter: If this lesson needs to be divided into two presentations, this may be a good place to stop and continue in a later session.

C.  **Resistance to change:** Deep down, many people find that there are many parts of themselves and their addictive lifestyles they really don't want to let go. Here are some ways others have successfully tackled this problem:

1.  *"I want to want to":* If people can't honestly say they want to change something, at least they can often say they wished they wanted to change. That's a good start; they can keep working on it.

2.  *Accept the feelings, but control the actions:* Sometimes a person can't leave a character trait behind as long as he or she is trying to get rid of it. Controlling the urge to act on it may be all that's possible for a while. That's okay. Once the characteristic is accepted with the hope that it can be changed soon and the view that he or she is okay at that point for that day, it often does start changing.

3.  *Find replacement activities:* Often it isn't the chemical or addictive behavior itself that the addict craves but something else that happened when he or she consumed it. The solution is to find new ways to get that other effect, to figure out what the payoff was and find another way to get it without such a high price tag.

4.  *Set small goals and reward yourself:* This is a good way to build new habits. It takes about three weeks of practice for most people to get a new habit formed. Plan for small rewards several times during that period for sticking to it. Give this change time!

5.  *Hang around with people who are the way the newly recovering person wants to be:* Newcomers learn by example, and some of these old-timers' attitudes and habits may rub off.

D.  **Anger, fear, and hopelessness/depression:** One of the reasons addicts use and drink is to block negative emotions; and when they quit, it can seem as if they're spinning out of control. To get through this phase, the newly sober person may try some of these approaches:

1. *Talk about the feelings:* With a trusted friend or at a good meeting, talking about these feelings helps the new person understand them better and feel more peaceful, and chances are someone else will say "me, too!" and add some insights that may help even further.

2. *Take care of oneself:* Eating a healthy diet, getting enough sleep, and getting regular exercise in enjoyable forms will all help cope with these emotions and make them more manageable.

3. *At least one good laugh a day:* Hearty laughter changes brain chemistry the same way as getting strenuous exercise. As with some prescription drugs, it releases natural antidepressants and painkillers, with no side effects. It may help to collect some comedy videos or books and turn to them on a difficult day.

4. *Look out for distorted thinking:* Think out loud and get feedback from a friend, or listen to yourself and figure out what beliefs are behind the negative feelings. Often people realize that they are trying to live up to impossible rules and expectations they haven't really thought about. When they get these rules and expectations into conscious awareness and take a close look at them, many negative feelings may go away.

5. *Get some counseling:* See a therapist. He or she may be able to help in getting past the negative feelings.

6. *Give this some time:* These feelings are a normal, but temporary, part of recovery, and don't last as long as they seem to. People have been emotionally numb, and now things are coming back to life. Guide the group in thinking about what happens when a leg goes to sleep, then gets its circulation back—it hurts and feels crazy, but only for a short time.

**E.** **Relationships with people (significant others, family, friends, supervisors, and coworkers):** Some of these people may be very angry, hurt, and suspicious because of the newly sober person's past actions; they may like the addict better sick and undermine his or her recovery; or they may just not understand and may cause problems for that reason. Often they are trying to decide whether to stay in these relationships; and when they see the addict start changing, it's both hopeful and frightening for them. They may also have their own drug and alcohol problems, which make another person's recovery seem threatening. These are some time-tested solutions to these relationship problems:

1. *Listen to them and let them vent:* Give them a chance to say how they feel about whatever may have happened. Don't argue, explain, or defend: The recovering person should just listen closely, then tell them what he or she believes they said. They will either agree, disagree and correct, or stay mad and keep blasting. The key is to keep listening and reflecting back and checking for understanding; and they will run out of steam, usually fairly quickly, and become more open to noticing the changes in the recovering addict, who can then explain his or her view if necessary.

2. *Help them understand:* It helps to explain the recovery process and its principles to them, as far as it's safe to trust them with that information. If they knew about the addiction, the addict might as well tell them about the recovery. Give them the chance to read some literature about recovery. Invite them to come along to some open meetings.

3. *Encourage them if they seem interested (gently, in a nonpushy way) to get involved in their own recovery programs:* Such as Al-Anon, AlaTeen, CoDependents Anonymous, and so on.

4. *Make amends when the time is right and give them time:* As the newly sober person changes, most people

will eventually come around to seeing, accepting, and trusting that change. Some may not, but that is beyond your control.

5. *Don't be a victim:* Recovering people should not put themselves in situations where they are being used or abused or where their recovery is being undermined. It's important to avoid, change, or leave those situations.

F. **Work, money, and time-management problems:** These can seem overwhelming, especially when they require people to make major changes in their habits. It can be very difficult to adjust, especially when a newly sober addict's body is still withdrawing from a drug, the addict's schedule may be busier than it has ever been, and he or she is trying to juggle work with meetings and other activities. Here are some ways to make this easier:

1. *Have a consistent routine:* Make and follow a regular schedule. Structure lowers the stress level by reducing the number of decisions that must be made daily. If a person always gets up at the same time, he or she doesn't have to decide when to get up; if people always go to a meeting after work, they don't have to decide what to do at that time. Also, in a short time the new routine will become as strong a set of habits as the old one.

2. *Get help from others:* It helps to have other people both encouraging us and depending on us. Get a work-out partner, join a car pool, seek the advice of someone wise and trusted, get others (sponsor and program friends) to help by pointing out if they see the newly recovering member straying from the plan and when they see him or her doing well at it.

3. *Reward oneself for success:* Everyone should give themselves little rewards often as they score small victories. Mention them at meetings, go out for a walk, make a treat of a movie and dinner if possible—not only after accomplishing something great but also after

some of the "baby steps." And as always, allow some time to adjust.

4. *Get organized:* Get and use a notebook-type organizer, calendar, or filing system. Schedule regular times for things like paying the bills, balancing the checkbook, and so on. Make checklists for tasks. Set aside time at the beginning or end of the day to review what needs to be done or what has been done that day.

G. **Legal problems:** It is best to tackle legal problems head on and get them over with (and newly sober addicts often have no choice because the legal problems tackle them). As long as these are hanging over people's heads, they have a hard time relaxing and being comfortable with themselves, and their stress level stays higher than if the problems were dealt with. Recovering people who have legal problems should talk with their lawyers and do what is necessary to get the issues resolved. Sometimes willingness to face and deal with problems will make a strong, favorable impression on people and show them that you are changing, too.

H. **Health problems:** Hopefully, once the newly recovering person's body is drug-free, health problems will clear up quickly. If not, it's important to see a doctor and take appropriate self-care measures. If physical health is not good, it will make the rest of the recovery process more difficult. As recommended earlier, it's important to eat a healthy diet and get enough rest and exercise, and it's a good idea to have at least one good hearty laugh daily if possible.

I. **Switching addictions:** The underlying attraction of any addiction is its power to make people feel better very quickly. In addition to giving up a particular addictive behavior, a recovering person who wishes to stay free from other addictions must also learn to seek non-self-destructive ways to feel better. Otherwise he or she is likely to slip into a new addiction, often without realizing it. For example, many alcoholics and addicts who become chemically clean and sober develop problems with gambling, workaholism, or compulsive sexual behavior. To avoid this, the best approach is to proactively seek out healthy ways to reduce stress, cope with physical or emotional pain, and have fun. Many of those healthy methods have already been discussed in this lesson, such as talking with people, exercise, laughter, a healthy diet, rest, and so on.

## III. CONCLUSION:

A. **Summary:** This presentation briefly covered several common problems in early 12-step recovery along with effective coping skills to overcome those problems. This information is important because being able to make effective use of 12-step programs is a critical part of recovery for most people who succeed in achieving long-term sobriety from addictive behaviors.

B. **Review the learning goals:**

1. On completion of this presentation, group members will demonstrate knowledge of at least four common problems in early 12-step recovery.

2. On completion of this presentation, group members will demonstrate an understanding of at least one effective coping strategy for each of the problems listed for the first performance objective.

3. On completion of this presentation, group members will describe personal plans for practical application of solutions to common problems in early 12-step recovery.

C. **Questions/Discussion**

# THE 12 STEPS, RELATIONSHIPS, AND WORK

**DURATION:** 2 hours 0 minutes

**TARGET POPULATION:** Clients in treatment or early recovery from addictive disorders

**FACILITY REQUIRED:** Classroom with desks or chairs and tables

**MATERIAL AND EQUIPMENT REQUIRED:**

Flip chart pads and stand, white board, or chalkboard

Markers or chalk

Optional: Computer with LCD projector or overhead projector and screen

Handouts

**PERFORMANCE OBJECTIVES:** On completion of this presentation the participant will be able to:

1. Demonstrate awareness of the relationship between addictive lifestyles and problems with balance and boundaries in life.

2. Demonstrate understanding of at least three potential problems in balancing recovery, relationships, and work in early 12-step recovery.

3. Describe personal plans for avoiding or overcoming problems in balancing 12-step work, personal relationships, and work in early recovery.

**METHODS/TECHNIQUES OF INSTRUCTION:** Lecture and discussion

## I. INTRODUCTION:

A. **The subject and why it is important:** Ask group members to brainstorm and list problems they have experienced with balance and boundaries among areas of their lives when actively engaged in addictive behaviors, including discussion of what the term *boundaries* means to them in this context. Prompt them to briefly discuss why balance is a problem for people with addictive personalities. Write their answers on a board, flipchart, or transparency, using check marks to show duplicate answers. Referring back to the responses from the brainstorming session, ask the group how they think people in recovery do or should handle issues of balance differently than they did when they were actively practicing their addictions. Guide them in discussing how the potential problems identified might affect their own ability to stay clean and sober. Ask them to share any specific strategies they will use to avoid or overcome problems of balance in their lives. Tell the group that the information in this presentation is based on the experiences of many others who have been in the position that they are in now and is given to increase the group members' chances of success and help them achieve the best quality of life.

B. **Group policy (learning goals, policy on questions):** Explain to group members and advise them that they will be evaluated to check accomplishment of these goals.

1. *Learning goals:*

    (a) On completion of this presentation, group members will demonstrate awareness of the relationship between addictive lifestyles and problems with balance and boundaries in life.

    (b) On completion of this presentation, group members will demonstrate an understanding of at least three potential problems in balancing recovery, relationships, and work in early 12-step recovery.

    (c) On completion of this presentation, group members will describe personal plans to avoid or overcome problems in balancing 12-step work, personal relationships, and work in early recovery.

2. *Questions:* The instructor may either have group members hold their questions until the end of the presentation or ask questions spontaneously. If participation is a high priority, we recommend spontaneous questions; if brevity is more important, it works better to hold questions until the end.

## II. WHY BALANCE IS HARD FOR ADDICTS TO ACHIEVE:

**A. Poor judgment and impulse control when acting out:** When any human being uses alcohol or any other mind-altering chemical, the first parts of the brain that are affected are the portions used to make decisions and think about the future. This is the reason a depressant such as alcohol causes people to relax and stop worrying, at least for a short time. Other addictive behaviors have similar results because they trigger changes in brain chemistry similar to the effects of drugs. Regardless of whether the addiction is gambling, cocaine, or sex, engaging in the behavior changes the thinking processes in ways that make it difficult or impossible to stop when people continue to feel an urgent need to change the way they feel. As a result, addicts shortchange other parts of their lives to spend more of their time, money, and whatever else is needed to get the quick-fix feeling they believe they need.

B. **Tolerance and withdrawal:** Over time, it takes more of any addictive substance or behavior to give the addict the same effect, making it harder as time passes to maintain limits. Withdrawal is another part of addiction, causing distress (either physical or emotional) if the addict doesn't carry out the addictive behavior. So, even if he or she realizes it's costing too much, it's hard to hold back and save time, money, energy, and attention for other things.

C. **Family, peer group, and cultural values:** Addiction is a family illness. Most addicts learn addictive ways of thinking long before they begin their actual addictive behaviors, often during their childhoods. The family members and friends of many addicts tend to share such addictive behavior patterns as seeking instant gratification, behaving impulsively without much thought for long-term consequences, and overindulging in any pleasurable experience. Addicts who are just entering recovery may never have learned any other way to think and make decisions. This is what is often called *having an addictive personality.*

## III. POTENTIAL PROBLEMS WITH BALANCE IN EARLY RECOVERY:

A. **Tendency to go to extremes:** Addiction is sometimes called *the disease of more,* also known as the disease of *I want what I want and I want it now.* Those who have formed addictive thinking styles tend to go overboard in nearly everything they do. One of the most difficult things for addicts who are new in recovery to learn is to be content with enough of anything rather than pushing harder than is good for them. This makes it easy to get carried away with what they are doing at the moment and take any activity, even a healthy recovery-oriented one, to unhealthy extremes and neglect others in the process. Although it is important to make getting and staying sober the highest priority and devote a lot of time and attention to recovery, it is not good to put so much into this that it leads to neglecting serious responsibilities in other parts of life. That, in turn, can lead to becoming burned out on recovery and drifting into relapse.

B. **Demands and expectations from loved ones:** Since part of an addictive lifestyle is often neglect of the family, many addicts may tend to go overboard in trying to compensate for past failures. On one hand, this can cause problems when the family has gotten used to getting along without the addict being around much, and now the newly recovering person feels shut out. On the other hand, the family of a newly recovering addict may feel that he or she continues to neglect them to spend time with newfound friends and activities in recovery. There may be some truth to this, as some people get so absorbed in recovery programs that they give no more time to their families than when they were acting out their addictions.

C. **Expectations about work and financial pressures:** With work, too, it is easy to get carried away. Newly sober people want to repair damaged reputations, and they may also fall into workaholism, a pattern in which people lose themselves in work the way they may previously have lost themselves in drinking and drugging, as a way to numb uncomfortable feelings. If this happens, recovering addicts may put themselves under so much unhealthy pressure that they end up resenting the competing demands of both families and recovery programs.

## IV. WAYS TO AVOID OR OVERCOME PROBLEMS WITH BALANCE:

A. **Planning and scheduling:** As the cliché says, "No one plans to fail, but many people fail to plan." Because out-of-balance behavior is usually unintended, unplanned, and impulsive, one of the best ways to avoid it is to organize time to make sure recovery, important relationships, and work are all taken care of. It's wise to make a weekly schedule allowing time for meetings, work with a sponsor, prayer and meditation, work, exercise, rest, family or relationship time, and some time to relax alone. People new to recovery do well to make this type of schedule, keep it with them, and check it often to stay on track until new habits develop.

B. **Learning from role models:** Among people who achieve long-term recovery, many (not all) are good role models for balancing recovery with other important parts of life. This is one of the qualities a newly recovering person should look for when finding a sponsor, as well as when spending time with recovering people other than the sponsor. By watching and listening, asking questions, and using the skills modeled by these old-timers, newly recovering people can gain valuable insight that will help them "practice these principles in all their affairs."

C. **Support and feedback:** It's important for newly recovering people to have a support network of people who understand what they are doing and provide encouragement, suggestions, and feedback. For addicts who are getting clean and sober, a critical activity is to build support networks. This is done by listening to people share at meetings and seeking out those who have good solutions to life problems and by socializing with healthy recovering people and sharing experiences and concerns with them. It is also wise to talk with trusted people who are close to the addicts, explaining what the addicts are trying to do, and getting their frequent feedback on whether it looks to them as if the addicts are following through on the principles and plans they have shared with them. Part of many recovery and relapse prevention plans is a list of such people and a schedule for talking with them.

## V. CONCLUSION:

A. **Summary:** This presentation briefly covered reasons people with addictive personalities often have problems with balance and boundaries in life, some potential problems with balance in early recovery, and some strategies for avoiding or overcoming those problems. This information is important because being able to achieve balance and maintain healthy boundaries among important areas in life is vital to successful recovery for most people with addictive personalities.

B. **Review the learning goals:**

1. On completion of this presentation, group members will demonstrate awareness of the relationship between addictive lifestyles and problems with balance and boundaries in life.

2. On completion of this presentation, group members will demonstrate an understanding of at least three potential problems to balance recovery, relationships, and work in early 12-step recovery.

3. On completion of this presentation, group members will describe personal plans to avoid or overcome problems in balancing 12-step work, personal relationships, and work in early recovery.

C. **Questions/Discussion**

# THE 12 STEPS AND FINANCIAL SELF-MANAGEMENT

**DURATION:** 2 hours 0 minutes

**TARGET POPULATION:** Clients in treatment or early recovery from addictive disorders

**FACILITY REQUIRED:** Classroom with desks or chairs and tables

**MATERIAL AND EQUIPMENT REQUIRED:**

Flip chart pads and stand, white board, or chalkboard

Markers or chalk

Optional: Computer with LCD projector or overhead projector and screen

Handouts

**PERFORMANCE OBJECTIVES:** On completion of this presentation the participant will be able to:

1. Demonstrate awareness of the relationship between addictive lifestyles and problems with personal financial management.

2. Demonstrate understanding of at least three potential financial problem areas in early 12-step recovery.

3. Describe personal plans for avoiding or overcoming personal financial problems in early recovery.

**METHODS/TECHNIQUES OF INSTRUCTION:** Lecture and discussion

## I. INTRODUCTION:

A. **The subject and why it is important:** Ask group members to brainstorm and list problems they experienced with financial self-management when actively engaged in addictive behaviors. Prompt them to briefly discuss underlying reasons why financial responsibility is a problem for people with addictive personalities, and how financial difficulties in turn might make it harder to stay clean and sober. Write their answers on a board, flipchart, or transparency, using check marks to show duplicate answers. Referring back to the responses from the brainstorming session, ask the group how they think people in recovery do or should handle their personal finances differently than they did when they were actively practicing their addictions. Guide them in discussing how the potential financial problems identified might affect their own ability to stay clean and sober. Ask them to share any specific strategies they will use to avoid or overcome financial problems in their lives. Tell the group that the information in this presentation is based on the experiences of many others who have been in the position that they are in now and is given to increase the group members' chances of success and help them achieve the best quality of life.

B. **Group policy (learning goals, policy on questions):** Explain to group members and advise them that they will be evaluated to check accomplishment of these goals.

   1. *Learning goals:*

      (a) On completion of this presentation, group members will demonstrate awareness of the relationship between addictive lifestyles and problems with personal financial management.

     (b) On completion of this presentation, group members will demonstrate an understanding of at least three potential financial problem areas in early 12-step recovery.

     (c) On completion of this presentation, group members will describe personal plans to avoid or overcome personal financial problems in early recovery.

2. *Questions:* The instructor may either have group members hold their questions until the end of the presentation or ask questions spontaneously. If participation is a high priority, we recommend spontaneous questions; if brevity is more important, it works better to hold questions until the end.

## II. WHY RESPONSIBLE FINANCIAL MANAGEMENT IS HARD FOR ADDICTS TO ACHIEVE:

**A. Family values and lack of effective financial skills and habits:** Many people with addictions come from families in which their parents also suffered from addictions or other problems that prevented them from functioning effectively as parents. In the area of personal financial management, parental role modeling is the only training many people get in our society. Most school systems don't teach students how to balance checkbooks, manage credit, save money, or shop wisely. Those in the group whose parents' financial behavior was marked by impulsiveness, recklessness, and distorted priorities are likely to have learned and practiced the same patterns. In addition, most people who were raised by addicted parents learned addictive ways of thinking and acting in general, such as seeking instant gratification and overindulging in pleasurable experiences.

**B. Impaired judgment and impulse control:** Whenever people engage in addictive behaviors, either abusing substances or otherwise, their brain chemistry is changed in ways that impairs their ability to make sound decisions and refrain from acting on urges. Combined with access to credit cards, ATMs, or other means of getting and spending money quickly, this is a recipe for loss of financial control.

C. **The cost of addiction itself:** Many addictions become very expensive, especially those involving illicit drugs, gambling, compulsive spending, and acting out sexually. In the grip of an addiction, it is easy to allow spending to exceed income by huge amounts, so that an addict entering early recovery and taking stock of his or her life often realizes that one of the aftereffects of active addiction is a crushing burden of debt that may take years to resolve.

D. **Impaired earning power:** While most addicts of all kinds are highly productive and have excellent earning capacity when clean and sober, the later stages of addiction rob them of these things and make it difficult for them to keep jobs because of absenteeism, showing up at work impaired, conflict with coworkers, and other changes.

## III. POTENTIAL FINANCIAL PROBLEMS IN EARLY RECOVERY:

A. **Tendency to become overwhelmed:** Especially at first, newly recovering people tend to become anxious and depressed when they think about their financial situations. It's easy to begin feeling hopeless and to have second thoughts about the recovery process.

B. **Difficulties with health and employability:** Many people are quite ill and fragile—physically, mentally, and emotionally—for some time after they enter recovery. Together with the poor reputations they may have created during the period of their addictive acting out, this may make it difficult or impossible to find gainful employment for some time, in many cases several months or even a year or more.

C. **Demands and expectations from loved ones:** The addictive lifestyle often includes neglect of the family, including financial neglect. When a newly recovering person begins trying to change his or her life, the family may respond with years' worth of pent-up anger and unreasonable demands. However, many addicts are the source of their own unreasonable demands. In their desire to make up for the harms they have done to their loved ones, they may plunge into workaholic behavior. This can lead to neglect of basic self-care, attending to family in other ways, and the activities necessary to stay clean and sober and progress in recovery.

D. **Self-expectations about amends:** A common tendency of people in early 12-step recovery is to get ahead of themselves in working the steps, and the most common form of this mistake is in undertaking an ambitious process of making amends—Step 9—before working through the previous 8 steps. Especially for a person who still hasn't learned much about restraint, it's easy to overcommit on amends just as he or she may have previously overdone things in other ways. While it is necessary to make financial amends, it is important to do this at the right time.

## IV. WAYS TO AVOID OR OVERCOME PROBLEMS WITH FINANCIAL SELF-MANAGEMENT:

A. **Apply the steps:** The admission of powerlessness and unmanageability in Step 1 applies to all aspects of life, including finances. It may be very useful to substitute the phrase "my finances" for "alcohol" or whatever other word or phrase is included in the steps as practiced by each person's recovery program. Once this admission of powerlessness and unmanageability is made, the next two steps guide the newly recovering person in turning this problem over to the Higher Power of his or her understanding and becoming willing to follow whatever guidance is given.

Most often this guidance is to do the next right thing and pay attention to the directions and advice of sponsors and other role models, which leads to the next item.

B. **Learn from 12-step role models:** A sponsor and others who have achieved long-term recovery are likely to have had financial problems of their own and can share their experience in regaining financial sanity. This is an important consideration in finding a sponsor, as well as spending time with recovering people other than the sponsor, because some "old-timers" have merely switched addictions and become compulsive spenders or gamblers after giving up chemical addictions. By watching and listening, asking questions, and using the skills modeled by the long-time sober people who do practice sober financial habits, people who are new to recovery can learn and emulate effective strategies to regain and keep control of their personal finances.

C. **Budget and plan:** To avoid impulsive spending and use money wisely, it's a good idea for a newly recovering person to make a personal budget, plan his or her spending, and follow the budget. It may help to share this information with another recovering person and ask that other person to monitor compliance with the budget. In addition, the newly recovering person will find that he or she can save money by planning meals and making grocery lists accordingly, shopping ahead of time to avoid buying things at higher priced convenience stores, packing sack lunches instead of eating at fast food restaurants, and avoiding shopping when hungry.

D. **Avoid credit:** Many people in recovery, both those who are newly clean and sober and many who aren't, find it best to avoid having credit cards. One ATM debit card can usually be used for any purchase that would otherwise require a credit card. This makes it impossible to go into debt on impulse.

E. **Take it one day at a time:** To avoid becoming overwhelmed in this area as in others, it is important to keep the focus on today. It may be useful for the newly recovering person to post notes or other reminders in places where he or she will see them often as reminders to concentrate on what can be done today rather than pointlessly worrying about past events that can't be changed or future events that cannot yet be affected.

F. **Seek out support and feedback:** As in other areas, it is vital for a newly recovering person to have an emotional and spiritual support network to provide support, encouragement, and feedback. For the person entering recovery, building a support network is a high priority. It's crucial to go to meetings and listen to people, to seek out those who are practicing the principles of 12-step recovery in all areas of their lives, and share concerns, challenges, experiences, and ideas with them.

## V. CONCLUSION:

A. **Summary:** This presentation briefly covered reasons that people with addictive personalities often have problems with financial self-management, some potential financial problem areas in early recovery, and some strategies for preventing or coping with those problems. This can be vital in avoiding relapse because financial stress is second only to relationship problems as a trigger for relapse into addictions.

B. **Review the learning goals:**

1. On completion of this presentation, group members will demonstrate awareness of the relationship between addictive lifestyles and problems with personal financial management.

2. On completion of this presentation, group members will demonstrate an understanding of at least three

potential financial problem areas in early 12 step recovery.

3. On completion of this presentation, group members will describe personal plans to avoid or overcome personal financial problems in early recovery.

## C. Questions/Discussion

# THE 12 STEPS AND EMOTIONAL AND MENTAL PROBLEMS

**DURATION:** 2 hours 0 minutes

**TARGET POPULATION:** Clients in treatment or early recovery from addictive disorders

**FACILITY REQUIRED:** Classroom with desks or chairs and tables

**MATERIAL AND EQUIPMENT REQUIRED:**

Flip chart pads and stand, white board, or chalkboard

Markers or chalk

Optional: Computer with LCD projector or overhead projector and screen

Handouts

**PERFORMANCE OBJECTIVES:** On completion of this presentation the participant will be able to:

1.  Demonstrate awareness of the relationship between addictive lifestyles and emotional and mental problems frequently experienced as co-occurring disorders.

2.  Demonstrate understanding of at least three potential emotional or mental problems in early 12-step recovery.

3.  Describe personal plans for avoiding or coping with emotional and mental problems in early recovery.

**METHODS/TECHNIQUES OF INSTRUCTION:** Lecture and discussion

## I. INTRODUCTION:

A. **The subject and why it is important:** Ask group members to brainstorm and list emotional and mental problems often experienced by people with addictions or discuss problems the group members are experiencing. Prompt them to briefly discuss underlying relationships among these problems and how addiction might contribute to emotional or mental problems and vice versa. Write their answers on a board, flipchart, or transparency, using check marks to show duplicate answers. Referring back to the responses from the brainstorming session, ask the group how they think emotional and mental problems affect people who have gotten into recovery differently than they did when they were actively practicing their addictions. Guide them in discussing how addictive lifestyles may contribute to psychiatric problems and also how having mental and emotional problems may make a person more susceptible to addiction or make their addictions worse. Ask them to share any specific strategies they will use to avoid or overcome emotional and mental problems in their lives. Tell the group that the information in this presentation is based on the experiences of many others who have been in the position that they are in now and is given to increase the group members' chances of success and help them achieve the best quality of life.

B. **Group policy (learning goals, policy on questions):** Explain to group members and advise them that they will be evaluated to check accomplishment of these goals.

   1. *Learning goals:*

      (a) On completion of this presentation, group members will demonstrate awareness of the relationship between addictive lifestyles and emotional and mental problems frequently experienced as co-occurring disorders.

(b) On completion of this presentation, group members will demonstrate an understanding of at least three potential emotional or mental problems in early 12-step recovery.

(c) On completion of this presentation, group members will describe personal plans to avoid or cope with emotional and mental problems in early recovery.

2. *Questions:* The instructor may either have group members hold their questions until the end of the presentation or ask questions spontaneously. If participation is a high priority, we recommend spontaneous questions; if brevity is more important, it works better to hold questions until the end.

## II. HOW ADDICTIVE LIFESTYLES CONTRIBUTE TO EMOTIONAL AND MENTAL PROBLEMS AND VICE VERSA:

A. **Addiction increasing the likelihood of emotional and mental problems:** Although heredity sometimes plays a large role in making people vulnerable to emotional and mental problems, these problems can also result from life experiences. For example, a person practicing an addictive lifestyle may be much more likely to suffer violence and other trauma that could cause him or her to develop posttraumatic stress disorder (PTSD). Prolonged use of stimulant drugs such as cocaine, amphetamine, and methamphetamine can cause structural changes in the brain that reduce the ability to experience happiness and make a person permanently prone to depression and anxiety. Many other types of substance abuse can cause brain or nervous system damage. Finally, when a person emerges from addiction and begins trying to get clean and sober, he or she may be facing severe life problems as a result of his or her previous lifestyle and may be vulnerable to depression and anxiety connected with those problems.

B. **Emotional and mental problems increasing the risk of addiction:** People suffering from such problems as depression, anxiety disorders, bipolar depression, and schizophrenia often experience very unpleasant thoughts and feelings and find that by self-medicating these symptoms with mood-altering substances they can get temporary relief. In the process of regularly self-medicating to relieve symptoms of emotional or mental distress, they may become physically and psychologically dependent on the substances they use for this.

C. **Predisposition to both types of problems:** As was mentioned earlier, heredity plays a role in many cases of emotional and mental problems. Depression, bipolar depression, and schizophrenia all run in families. The same is true of alcoholism and other addictions, and many of the families that are at higher risk for emotional and mental problems are the same families that are prone to addictions. For people who grow up with parents or other adult family members who are actively addicted or emotionally or mentally ill, the risk of developing these problems in their own adult lives may be increased further because of the effects of their childhood environments. For example, children raised by parents who abuse alcohol and other drugs are much more likely to do so themselves starting in early adolescence, and some emotional problems may be partially a matter of a learned way of thinking and responding.

## III. POTENTIAL EMOTIONAL AND MENTAL PROBLEMS IN EARLY RECOVERY:

A. **Depression, anxiety, and mood swings:** Long-term substance abuse causes major changes in the chemistry of the brain. The drugs mimic natural brain chemicals, making it seem to the body that these chemicals are present in excess.

The body tries to restore its natural balance by cutting back on production of the original natural brain chemicals. Drugs that speed up or slow down the metabolism cause the body to adapt by slowing down or speeding up to compensate. Although the drugs themselves may be out of the body within days or weeks after a person quits, these delicate balances in the brain and the rest of the body may take several months to return to normal. This period of being physically out of balance, known as Post-Acute Withdrawal Syndrome (PAWS), can include symptoms such as rapid mood swings and tendencies toward depression, anxiety, and irritability. Combined with the natural anxiety and depression newly recovering people experience in facing the accumulated consequences of their addictive lifestyles, this can lead to mood problems that increase the risk of relapse, especially when they continue for months, and the newly recovering person fears that they are permanent.

B. **Lack of alternative coping skills for emotional pain:** A common experience in the first year or two of recovery is that of feeling all emotions more intensely than ever before because the newly clean and sober person is no longer numbing them. When the feelings are pleasant, it is often called the *pink-cloud experience.* However, life inevitably includes loss and pain; and in addition, a new loss may trigger re-experiencing of old losses that the person never processed emotionally when they took place. When the now-sober addict faces bereavement, divorce, major health problems, or other painful situations, and a possible cascade of unresolved pain accompanying the current distress, with his or her feelings un-anesthetized for the first time; he or she is often unprepared for the intensity of the feelings and may feel tempted to return to drinking or drugging to cope.

C. **Problems with memory, sleep, and attention:** Other aspects of PAWS include difficulties with short-term memory, insomnia, and problems sustaining attention; all of which may persist for several months. These problems make the newly recovering person's daily life more difficult. Like the mood swings described earlier, they can also cause the sufferer to fear that these changes are permanent because they last for months after the last drink or drug use. It is important to realize that these things will pass with time if the person stays clean and sober. While they endure, however, they can also disrupt the practice of healthy habits being cultivated as part of recovery, such as daily prayer and meditation; calling a sponsor at a set time daily; or maintaining a healthy routine of diet, exercise, and rest.

## IV. WAYS TO AVOID OR COPE WITH EMOTIONAL AND MENTAL PROBLEMS IN EARLY RECOVERY:

A. **Comply with treatment:** Along with beginning active participation in a 12-step recovery program, it is vital for a newly clean and sober person to comply with any psychotherapeutic, psychiatric, and general medical treatment he or she is receiving. This includes taking prescribed medications, exactly as the prescribing physician directs. For clarification of questions about the interrelationship between psychotherapy, medication, and 12-step recovery, see Exercise II-Z and Section IV of this book and the pamphlet titled "The A.A. Member: Medications and Other Drugs" published by Alcoholics Anonymous World Services, Inc. The official stance of AA and other 12-step programs is that if a person is working with a physician who is experienced with addictions, has told that physician about his or her addiction, and is taking the medication exactly as prescribed, that person is doing the right thing. This can be a matter of life or death because noncompliance can lead to suicidal depression, life-threatening manic episodes, or psychotic experiences that can endanger the life of the sufferer or others.

**B. Practice good self-care:** As much as possible, the newly clean and sober person should eat a healthy diet, get a moderate amount (20–30 minutes) of cardiovascular exercise daily, try to get some fresh air, and get a healthy amount of sleep. Although PAWS may include insomnia, as noted earlier, a regular exercise routine makes it easier to sleep at night, provided the exercise is completed several hours before bedtime.

**C. Applying the steps:** The admission of powerlessness and unmanageability in Step 1 applies to thoughts and feelings as well as the primary addiction. The newly sober person should try substituting the phrase "my thoughts and feelings" for the word or phrase included in the steps as adapted to each 12-step program. Steps 2 and 3 will guide the newly recovering addict in turning these painful thoughts and emotions over to a Higher Power of his or her understanding and becoming willing to be guided in handling them. The best way to ask for and follow this guidance is to seek an understanding of what is the next right thing to do and to listen to sponsors and other role models.

**D. Learn from others:** A newly sober person who is suffering from depression, anxiety, fear, irritability, confusion, or other difficult feelings is not alone. By sharing these feelings with others in his or her 12-step group, in individual conversations or in a meeting, he or she can get support, encouragement, and often practical feedback on how others have successfully coped with these emotional and mental problems.

**E. Take it one day at a time:** Sometimes the most useful of the many 12-step slogans are "One day at a time" and "This, too, shall pass." Many old-timers will advise the newcomer that "one day at a time" may become "one hour at a time" or "one minute at a time" depending on the difficulty of the stressor being experienced. The key is to keep your focus on the present and on getting through the challenges of the moment.

## V. CONCLUSION:

**A. Summary:** This presentation briefly covered reasons people with addictive personalities often have emotional and mental problems and vice versa, some potential emotional and mental problems in early recovery, and strategies for preventing or coping with those problems. As with other lessons in this series, this information can be vital in early recovery, as emotional and mental distress is a frequent trigger for relapse into addiction.

**B. Review the learning goals:**

1. On completion of this presentation, group members will demonstrate awareness of the relationship between addictive lifestyles and emotional and mental problems frequently experienced as co-occurring disorders.

2. On completion of this presentation, group members will demonstrate an understanding of at least three potential emotional or mental problems in early 12-step recovery.

3. On completion of this presentation, group members will describe personal plans to avoid or cope with emotional and mental problems in early recovery.

**C. Questions/Discussion**

# THE 12 STEPS AND SOCIAL LIFE

**DURATION:** 2 hours 0 minutes

**TARGET POPULATION:** Clients in treatment or early recovery from addictive disorders

**FACILITY REQUIRED:** Classroom with desks or chairs and tables

**MATERIAL AND EQUIPMENT REQUIRED:**

Flip chart pads and stand, white board, or chalkboard

Markers or chalk

Optional: Computer with LCD projector or overhead projector and screen

Handouts

**PERFORMANCE OBJECTIVES:** On completion of this presentation the participant will be able to:

1.  Demonstrate awareness of the relationship between addictive lifestyles and problems with social relationships.

2.  Demonstrate understanding of at least three potential problems with social life in early 12-step recovery.

3.  Describe personal plans for creating a healthy social life in early recovery.

**METHODS/TECHNIQUES OF INSTRUCTION:** Lecture and discussion

## I. INTRODUCTION:

A. **The subject and why it is important:**  Ask group members to brainstorm and list problems with social life that are often experienced by people with addictions or discuss problems the group members are experiencing. Prompt them to briefly discuss the connections between these problems and active addictions, and how addiction might contribute to social problems and vice versa. Write their answers on a board, flipchart, or transparency, using check marks to show duplicate answers. Referring back to the responses from the brainstorming session, ask the group how they think the social lives of people who get clean and sober change in comparison to the way they were when they were actively practicing their addictions. Guide them in discussing how addictive lifestyles may contribute to social problems and also how the friendships and social habits they've had in the past might have contributed to their addictive problems and, if unchanged, might make them more susceptible to relapse. Ask them to share any specific strategies they will use to avoid or overcome social problems in their lives now that they are working to stay clean and sober. Tell the group that the information in this presentation is based on the experiences of many others who have been in the position that they are in now and is given to increase the group members' chances of success and help them achieve the best quality of life.

B. **Group policy (learning goals, policy on questions):**  Explain to group members and advise them that they will be evaluated to check accomplishment of these goals.

1. *Learning goals:*

   (a) On completion of this presentation, group members will demonstrate awareness of the relationship between addictive lifestyles and problems with social relationships.

(b) On completion of this presentation, group members will demonstrate an understanding of at least three potential problems with social life in early 12-step recovery.

(c) On completion of this presentation, group members will describe personal plans for creating a healthy social life in early recovery.

2. *Questions:* The instructor may either have group members hold their questions until the end of the presentation or ask questions spontaneously. If participation is a high priority, we recommend spontaneous questions; if brevity is more important, it works better to hold questions until the end.

## II. HOW ADDICTIVE LIFESTYLES CONTRIBUTE TO SOCIAL PROBLEMS AND VICE VERSA:

A. **Addiction increasing the likelihood of destructive friendships and social patterns:** When a person's life centers around an addiction, most of his or her relationships also become centered around that addiction. Most of the addict's interpersonal activities are with drinking and using buddies or others who share a particular addiction, and relationships with others who don't share this lifestyle are neglected or abandoned. Also, some common patterns in many addictions include dishonesty, secretiveness, mood swings, undependability, self-pity, blaming one's problems on others, and exploiting or taking advantage of others who are vulnerable because they are in close relationships with the addict. All these behavior patterns tend to alienate family members and friends who are not part of the addictive lifestyle. If the addictive lifestyle continues for long enough, the addict will usually be left with no relationships other than those based on the addictive pattern that dominates his or her life.

B. **Destructive relationships and social patterns increasing the risk and severity of addiction and relapse:** Most people with addictions were introduced to their addictive behaviors of choice by friends or family members. Once they have become abusers or addicts, these destructive patterns are usually reinforced by the addictive social networks described earlier. After they hit bottom and choose to become clean and sober, many people in early recovery find that their old friends will try to undermine their sobriety and persuade them to return to addiction, for any of a number of motives. Even if the old companions in addictive behavior don't actively pressure the newly clean and sober person to relapse, being around them as they continue to live the addictive lifestyle is likely to increase the difficulty of staying in recovery. The newly recovering addict will be exposed to sights, sounds, and smells that may be strong triggers for cravings and urges to relapse, and the old friends are likely to continue to practice their addictive behavior patterns, which are incompatible with recovery. One of the most common pieces of advice that 12-step program old-timers give to newcomers is to change their playpens and playmates, that is, stay away from their old haunts and their old friends and form new bonds with people living healthy lifestyles.

C. **Predisposition to both addiction and dysfunctional social relationships:** As we have noted elsewhere, addictive thinking and behavior tends to be a family pattern. People raised by parents who are behaving addictively grow up experiencing the unhealthy lifestyles and relationships of their primary role models as normal. In adolescence and adult life, they are much more likely to form similar patterns in life than people whose parents modeled healthy and functional behavior and relationship styles. For many people whose experience fits this description, part of recovery must include learning what those healthy patterns look like and how to practice them.

## III. POTENTIAL PROBLEMS WITH SOCIAL LIFE IN EARLY RECOVERY:

A. **Returning to old people, places, and patterns:** Long-time habits are hard to break. Unless they are careful, newly recovering people may find themselves falling back into their former lifestyles without even realizing they're doing it. They may also feel reluctant to give up old friendships, recreational habits, and hangouts. Being new in sobriety can be lonely and frightening, and the yearning for anything familiar is stronger. Old friends may be actively trying to get the newcomer to recovery to rejoin them. However, many who have relapsed have felt afterward that trying to change one part of their lives (their actual addictive behaviors) while keeping the associated relationships and habits was too difficult for them. In AA and the other 12-step programs, old-timers use the word *slippery* to refer to people, places, or activities that are invitations to return to active addiction. One of the pieces of advice most frequently heard in meetings is to stay away from slippery situations, or as some people put it, "If you don't want to fall down, don't do aerobics on the ice."

B. **Lack of healthy social skills and activities:** As we said earlier, a common problem of people raised by parents with addictive problems is that they never had healthy role models to teach them social styles that weren't self-destructive. Many alcoholics and addicts also say that they stopped growing up emotionally when they started their heavy drinking, drug use, or other addictive behaviors. This means that they went through many normal developmental stages and activities in an impaired condition. They may never have done many things sober, such as engaging in hobbies, going to parties, dating, dancing, and having sex. All of these activities, which may be part of the healthy relationships and social life the newly clean and sober person is trying to create, can be uncomfortable and even terrifying to a person who has never done them sober before.

C.  **Problems with moods, health, and money:**  Many people enter recovery in poor condition physically, mentally, emotionally, spiritually, legally, and financially. It may be very taxing to them to try to learn and practice new skills, attitudes, and activities when just getting through the day seems to be all they can handle. Yet, it is important to avoid becoming isolated and to build a healthy support network. Doing this while feeling tired, sick, shaky, depressed, anxious, irritable, and confused, while under financial stress that may be making it hard to pay for even basic necessities, is challenging.

## IV. WAYS TO AVOID OR COPE WITH SOCIAL PROBLEMS IN EARLY RECOVERY:

A.  **Apply the steps:**  As we note in other lessons and homework assignments, the steps can be used to handle many situations other than the specific addiction that a person is trying to overcome. When facing urges to return to old patterns or fear about trying new ones, the first three steps can be very useful. A person can substitute these problems for the addiction in Step 1, acknowledging that he or she is powerless over an urge, a thought, an emotion, or the actions of others and that his or her turmoil in response to this is making life unmanageable. Step 2 offers hope with the reflection that the Higher Power of a person's understanding can bring sanity and order back to his or her life. With Step 3, the invitation to turn the problem over to that Higher Power and do whatever is the next right thing as best it can be determined can relieve much of the pressure and fear that the newly recovering person may be feeling. In the passage frequently referred to as the "Promises" on pages 83 and 84 of AA's Big Book, this relief is described in two sentences: "We will intuitively know how to handle situations which used to baffle us. We will suddenly realize that God is doing for us what we could not do for ourselves."

B. **Stick with winners:** Another common piece of 12-step advice, this means that the newcomer should make a point of spending time with more experienced program members who are not only staying sober but have their lives in good order and balance. If the recently clean and sober person has chosen well in picking a sponsor, that sponsor will be one of these winners, and there will be others as well. Many newcomers—especially when their health or other circumstances prevent them from working in their first weeks or months of recovery—spend most of their waking hours at meetings or socializing with others in recovery.

C. **Participate in 12-step program social activities:** Many groups have frequent social functions ranging from dances to picnics to bingo nights. Frequently, 12-step meeting clubs will often host marathon or round-the-clock meetings on holidays, providing extra support at what can be more difficult times to stay sober. In addition, most 12-step programs hold conferences or conventions, in some cases fairly frequently. Whenever the newcomer attends a meeting or visits a 12-step club, he or she can look at the bulletin board and take note of upcoming events and make plans to participate. It may help to ask others whether they will also be going to events and make plans together with those who will also be attending.

D. **Take it one day at a time:** As with other issues, it can be helpful to keep the focus on the present day or the present hour. It is easier to accept uncomfortable feelings with the knowledge that they will pass in time and that all the newcomer has to do is stay sober, practice good self-care as much as possible, work the steps, and wait for things to change. Here again, talking with more experienced members about their experiences will help, as they relate how they felt the same way early in their recoveries and how things got better with time and work.

## V. CONCLUSION:

A. **Summary:** This presentation briefly covered reasons people with addictive personalities often have problems with relationships and social life and vice versa, some potential problems with social life in early recovery, and strategies for preventing or coping with those problems. As with other lessons in this series, this information can be vital in early recovery, as emotional and mental distress is a frequent trigger for relapse into addiction.

B. **Review the learning goals:**

1. On completion of this presentation, group members will demonstrate awareness of the relationship between addictive lifestyles and problems with social relationships.

2. On completion of this presentation, group members will demonstrate understanding of at least three potential problems with social life in early 12-step recovery.

3. On completion of this presentation, group members will describe personal plans for creating a healthy social life in early recovery.

C. **Questions/Discussion**

# 12-STEP RELAPSE-PREVENTION TOOLS

**DURATION:** 2 hours 0 minutes

**TARGET POPULATION:** Clients in treatment or early recovery from addictive disorders

**FACILITY REQUIRED:** Classroom with desks or chairs and tables

**MATERIAL AND EQUIPMENT REQUIRED:**

Flip chart pads and stand, white board, or chalkboard

Markers or chalk

Optional: Computer with LCD projector or overhead projector and screen

Handouts

**PERFORMANCE OBJECTIVES:** On completion of this presentation the participant will be able to:

1. Demonstrate understanding of at least three 12-step program practices or resources that are useful as relapse prevention tools.

2. Describe personal plans for using at least three 12-step program relapse prevention tools in his or her person recovery and relapse prevention planning.

**METHODS/TECHNIQUES OF INSTRUCTION:** Lecture and discussion

## I. INTRODUCTION:

A. **The subject and why it is important:** Ask group members to briefly discuss their thoughts and concerns about avoiding relapse into their addictions, then ask them to brainstorm and list methods and resources that might help them prevent relapse in their own recovery programs. Write their answers on a board, flipchart, or transparency, using check marks to show duplicate answers. Referring back to the responses from the brainstorming session, ask the group what kinds of triggers and problems cause most relapses. Go to the list of relapse-prevention tools the group identified and ask them to match these tools with the problems they have named and talk briefly about why they believe these tools would help with these problems. Ask whether they have seen or heard of long-time members from their 12-step groups using these tools and how they worked for those people.

B. **Group policy (learning goals, policy on questions):** Explain to group members and advise them that they will be evaluated to check accomplishment of these goals.

1. *Learning goals:*

   (a) On completion of this presentation, group members will demonstrate an understanding of at least three 12-step program practices or resources that are useful as relapse-prevention tools.

   (b) On completion of this presentation, group members will describe personal plans for using at least three 12-step program relapse-prevention tools in their person-recovery and relapse-prevention planning.

2. *Questions:* The instructor may either have group members hold their questions until the end of the presentation or ask questions spontaneously. If participation is a high priority, we recommend allowing spontaneous questions; if brevity is more important, it works better to hold questions until the end.

## II. USEFUL 12-STEP PROGRAM PRACTICES AND RESOURCES FOR AVOIDING RELAPSE:

A. **Attend meetings regularly and frequently and find a home group:** One of the most common pieces of advice newcomers to AA and other 12-step programs will probably hear is to attend at least 90 meetings during their first 90 days. Some newly recovering people, especially those with a lot of idle time on their hands because health or other problems make it hard for them to work at first, report that they benefit from attending several meetings a day during their first few months. Going to many meetings provides several benefits:

1. While at a meeting, the newcomer is in a safe place with no risk or opportunity to relapse.

2. Going to many meetings increases the rate of learning and absorption of the principles and practical application of the 12-step program. As one 12-step slogan puts it, "Repetition strengthens and confirms and faith becomes natural."

3. The more frequently a newcomer shares his or her own experiences, questions, and concerns at meetings, the more support and useful feedback he or she will get from others.

4. Increased contact with experienced group members, during meetings and in less formal interaction before and after meetings, helps the newcomer build a healthy social life and a strong interpersonal support network more quickly.

5. Going to meetings in several groups, and going to different types of meetings, such as open discussion, literature study, and speaker meetings, gives the newly recovering person a more complete experience of the 12-step program and the chance to learn which groups and types of meetings he or she finds most helpful.

6. While experiencing a variety of groups is good, it is also helpful to form a strong affiliation with one group. In this way, close bonds of trust and mutual understanding can be formed with members of that group, reducing the risk of emotional isolation and increasing the likelihood that if the newcomer is going astray emotionally others will know him or her well enough to see this, call it to the newly recovering person's attention, and offer support and help.

B. **Find a strong sponsor and work the steps:** While meetings are essential, they are not enough by themselves. By forming a relationship with a sponsor and working regularly and frequently with that sponsor (many sponsors ask their sponsees to call them daily and meet with them at least once per week), the newcomer gains intensive one-on-one support and a higher degree of accountability for diligently working on his or her recovery program. As a specific relapse prevention measure, it is useful for the newcomer to make a commitment to talk with the sponsor before engaging in addictive behavior in the event of a strong urge or craving. The sponsor will become the newcomer's mentor and guide in working the 12 steps. This is critical because many people who attend meetings but don't work the steps eventually relapse, and the newcomer will need the perspective and guidance of an experienced 12-step sponsor to work through the steps thoroughly and appropriately.

C. **Keep a phone list and meeting schedule handy:** Many old-timers will urge newcomers to take their telephone numbers and call anytime they are struggling in their new sobriety. It is a wise measure for any person new to 12-step recovery to keep a list of several other recovering people's phone numbers with him or her at all times. In addition, the 12-step communities in most places print schedules listing the days, times, locations, and meeting categories of all the meetings regularly scheduled in those cities or towns. The newcomer should also keep one of these meeting schedules handy. In some places, the meeting schedules are printed with a place to write phone numbers, allowing people to combine both these resources in a single piece of paper.

**D.** **Plan ahead to participate in 12-step activities at especially difficult times:** Each person new in recovery will find that some times are more difficult than others for him or her, though these will probably be different for every individual. For some people the tough times may be weekends, for others weeknights; holidays can be challenging, as can anniversaries of either happy or painful events. Knowing that a stressful event such as a court appearance, the first day on a new job, or a difficult personal encounter is pending can also trigger fears and urges to return to addictive patterns to escape painful feelings. For any of these situations, the newcomer can plan ahead. Specific plans work best. What meetings will they attend? In which 12-step social activities will they participate? If meetings or social gatherings are unavailable or insufficient, which program members will they talk to and arrange to spend time with?

**E.** **Practice regular prayer and meditation:** By making a regular practice of asking a personal Higher Power for help in staying sober and for guidance in daily decisions and actions, most recovering people report that they are able to maintain a more even and positive emotional state. When more stressful situations arise, praying for strength and guidance (see the recommendations earlier about applying the first three steps) often makes the difference between a challenging situation being experienced as too painful to handle without self-medication or as tough but tolerable. Meditation is useful for achieving and regaining calm and emotional balance and can be key in avoiding impulsive self-destructive behavior driven by strong emotions.

## III. INCORPORATING 12-STEP RELAPSE-PREVENTION TOOLS IN PERSONAL RECOVERY PLANNING:

A. **General planning:** A personal recovery plan should include both a routine for ordinary days and special plans for crises or difficult times. In the daily routine part of a personal recovery plan, the newcomer should seek to reduce his or her vulnerability to relapse by including practices that support stability. This is the place to schedule prayer, meditation, and meeting attendance, identify a home group, and plan regular step work with a sponsor.

B. **Crisis planning:** A personal recovery plan should also include concrete actions to be taken in a variety of types of crises. A good plan will include actions to handle both expected and unanticipated challenges and will also include some actions that involve the help of other people and some that the newcomer can take alone when no one else is available to help. This is where the lists of telephone numbers and meetings are important.

C. **Matching relapse prevention tools with problems:** Referring back to the specific problems and risk factors for relapse identified at the beginning of this lesson, each group member can examine his or her own life and decide which of the tools identified will be most helpful for each of the risk factors he or she may experience. For experience, a person who realizes that weekends will be the most difficult time to stay sober can concentrate on plans to attend more weekend meetings, meet with a sponsor on the weekend, and engage in social activities with other recovering people during the weekend. For another person, weekends may not be particularly difficult while holidays may be especially painful. This person would look through the list of tools and plan ways to use them on holidays throughout the year.

## IV. CONCLUSION:

A. **Summary:** This presentation briefly covered risk factors for relapse among people who are newly recovering in 12-step programs, some 12-step program activities and resources that are useful in reducing the risk of relapse, and ways to include these 12-step relapse-prevention tools in concrete and specific personal recovery and relapse prevention plans. As with other lessons in this series, this information can be vital in early recovery, as emotional and mental distress is a frequent trigger for relapse into addiction.

B. **Review the learning goals:**

1. On completion of this presentation, group members will demonstrate an understanding of at least three 12-step program practices or resources that are useful as relapse-prevention tools.

2. On completion of this presentation, group members will describe personal plans for using at least three 12-step program relapse-prevention tools in his or her person-recovery and relapse-prevention planning.

C. **Questions/Discussion**

# USEFUL BOOKS AND FILMS RELATED TO 12-STEP WORK

A number of widely available books and films can be helpful, both as references for the clinician incorporating 12-step work into addiction treatment and as homework assignments for clients. In addition to the books and films listed here, the book *Rent Two Films and Let's Talk in the Morning: Using Popular Movies in Psychotherapy, 2nd edition*, written by John W. and Jan T. Hesley and published by John Wiley & Sons, Inc., is a valuable reference. This book not only lists seven films with topics of substance abuse, two of which include 12-step work as a major part of their stories, it also catalogs dozens of other films that are useful in treating a range of other problems. As well as listing the films and matching them with problems, *Rent Two Films* includes detailed summaries and recommendations on how best to use them in psychotherapy.

Here are books on 12-step topics that may be useful, both as additions to an addiction treatment provider's professional library and as sources for reading assignments for clients:

*A.A. in Prison: Inmate to Inmate.* Alcoholics Anonymous World Services, Inc., 1991, 127 pages. This is a collection of personal stories from incarcerated alcoholics.

*Alcoholics Anonymous, 4th ed.* Alcoholics Anonymous World Services, Inc., 2001, 575 pages. The Big Book, the basic text of AA, explains the program and offers dozens of personal stories.

*Blueprint for Progress: Al-Anon's Fourth Step Inventory.* Al-Anon Family Group Headquarters, Inc., 1976, 61 pages. This is a structured, in-depth workbook for a Step-4 inventory on codependency and relationships.

*Clinician's Guide to the Twelve Step Principles.* Marvin D. Seppala, McGraw-Hill Medical Publishing Division, 2001, 208 pages. This book provides a discussion of the history and philosophy of the 12-step programs, with a step-by-step examination of the integration of spirituality and action.

*Co-Dependents Anonymous.* Co-Dependents Anonymous, Inc., 1995, 583 pages. This is the Big Book of Co-Dependents Anonymous.

*A Currency of Hope: Debtors Anonymous.* Debtors Anonymous General Service Office, 1999, 200 pages. This is the Big Book of Debtors Anonymous.

*A Design for Growth: How the Twelve Steps Work for Adult Children.* Veronica Ray, Hazelden, 1988, 112 pages. This is a guide to applying the steps for adult children of alcoholics.

*Emotions Anonymous.* Emotions Anonymous International, 1978, 251 pages. This is the Big Book of Emotions Anonymous.

*A Gentle Path through the Twelve Steps: A Guidebook for All People in the Process of Recovery.* Patrick Carnes, PhD, CompCare Publishers, 1989, 212 pages. This guidebook is suitable for applying the steps to any addiction, with many concrete questions and examples.

*Getting Started in A.A.* Hamilton B., Hazelden, 1995, 211 pages. This book provides one recovering person's extensive explanation of how AA works and detailed, concrete recommendations for newcomers.

*A Good First Step: A First Step Workbook for Twelve Step Programs.* Richard A. Hamel, CompCare Publishers, 1985, 89 pages. This workbook was written by a clinician, for an in-depth first step.

*Hope, Faith and Courage: Stories from the Fellowship of Cocaine Anonymous.* Cocaine Anonymous World Services, Inc., 1993, 217 pages. This book provides personal stories by cocaine addicts in recovery in this program.

*How Al-Anon Works for Families & Friends of Alcoholics.* Al-Anon Family Group Headquarters, Inc., 1995, 388 pages. This book provides basic, comprehensive descriptions of many aspects of that program and how it functions.

*Living Sober: Some Methods A.A. Members Have Used for Not Drinking.* Alcoholics Anonymous World Services, Inc., 1975, 88 pages. This book provides practical methods for coping with common challenges.

*Narcotics Anonymous, 5th ed.* Narcotics Anonymous World Services, Inc., 1988, 286 pages. This is the Big Book of Narcotics Anonymous, with an exceptionally clear discussion of addiction and recovery in the first five chapters.

*Overeaters Anonymous.* Overeaters Anonymous, Inc., 1980, 204 pages. This is the Overeaters Anonymous Big Book, with personal stories followed by appendixes explaining the program.

*Recovering Couples Anonymous: A Twelve Step Program for Couples, 3rd ed.* Recovering Couples Anonymous World Service Organization, 1996, 133 pages. This is the Big Book of this program, which is unique in its focus on couples and their relationships rather than on recovery on an individual basis.

*Sex and Love Addicts Anonymous.* The Augustine Fellowship, Sex and Love Addicts Anonymous, 1986, 280 pages. This is the Big Book of this program.

*Sharing Recovery through Gamblers Anonymous.* Gamblers Anonymous International Service Office, 1984, 228 pages. This is the Big Book of this program.

*A Skeptic's Guide to the Twelve Steps: What to Do When You Don't Believe.* Phillip Z., Hazelden, 1990, 241 pages. A psychologist and member of Overeaters Anonymous recounts how he overcame his resistance to spirituality to successfully recover using the steps.

*The Soul of Sponsorship: The Friendship of Fr. Ed Dowling, S. J. and Bill Wilson in Letters.* Robert Fitzgerald, S.J., Hazelden, 1995, 141 pages. This book is of interest for insight into the development and spiritual underpinnings of AA and the other 12-step programs.

*The Steps We Took.* Joe McQ., August House, 1990, 179 pages. This book provides detailed guidance on applying the steps from a clinician who has been studying and living by them for decades.

*There's More to Quitting Drinking than Quitting Drinking.* Dr, Paul O., Sabrina Publishing, 1995, 224 pages. This book is an exploration of moving beyond abstinence into mental and spiritual sobriety and recovery.

*The Twelve Steps: A Way Out, rev. ed.* Recovery Publications, 1986, 211 pages. This is a detailed workbook for adult children of dysfunctional families working the steps.

*Twelve Steps and Twelve Traditions.* Alcoholics Anonymous World Services, Inc., 1952, 192 pages. This book provides an in-depth exploration of the 12 steps and traditions.

*The Twelve Steps for Everyone Who Really Wants Them.* Hazelden, 1975, 141 pages. This book provides a guide for anyone working the steps in any program, with appendixes containing popular prayers.

*Understanding the Twelve Steps.* Terence T. Gorski, Simon & Schuster, 1989, 189 pages. This book is another clinician's perspective and explanation of the steps, applicable to any program.

Here are four films that may be useful for self-education and introducing clients to 12-step work. There are many more films addressing topics of substance abuse and treatment, but these are chosen because they focus on 12-step work in particular. These may be used either as homework assignments for clients, to be discussed in session afterward, or as presentations in treatment groups.

*\*Clean and Sober:* This film portrays a man who is addicted to cocaine and enters a 12-step based treatment program. His initial intent is to con his way through the program, but events lead him to realize that he truly needs to change and that he needs the steps to succeed.

*Inside Alcoholics Anonymous:* This is a documentary produced by the Arts and Entertainment network. It gives a well-organized overview of how AA works, including anonymous interviews with members of the program who describe their experiences.

*My Name Is Bill W:* This film tells the story of the founding of Alcoholics Anonymous by following Bill Wilson, one of the program's cofounders, through the depths of his alcoholic experience and then through the founding and first year or so of AA's existence.

*\*When a Man Loves a Woman:* In this film a woman who is an alcoholic enters a 12-step-based treatment program after a crisis in her family. She struggles with her overprotective husband's attempts to control and direct her recovery and his jealousy of her friendships with others in AA and her growing independence.

\*Also suggested in *Rent Two Films* for use in treating substance abuse.

This list is not complete by any means. Many of these books in turn recommend other books, and clinicians working in this area may find additional books and films that are useful through their own searching. Clients may provide information on new titles as well. If you have suggestions for books or films to add to those listed in this section, please give that information to the publisher for inclusion in future editions.

# THE 12 STEPS AND 12 TRADITIONS

## THE 12 STEPS OF ALCOHOLICS ANONYMOUS

1. We admitted we were powerless over alcohol—that our lives had become unmanageable.

2. Came to believe that a power greater than ourselves could restore us to sanity.

3. Made a decision to turn our will and our lives over to the care of God *as we understood Him.*

4. Made a searching and fearless moral inventory of ourselves.

5. Admitted to God, to ourselves, and to another human being the exact nature of our wrongs.

6. Were entirely ready to have God remove all these defects of character.

7. Humbly asked Him to remove our shortcomings.

8. Made a list of all persons we had harmed, and became willing to make amends to them all.

9. Made direct amends to such people wherever possible, except when to do so would injure them or others.

10. Continued to take personal inventory and when we were wrong promptly admitted it.

11. Sought through prayer and meditation to improve our conscious contact with God *as we understood Him,* praying only for knowledge of His will for us and the power to carry that out.

12. Having had a spiritual awakening as the result of these steps, we tried to carry this message to alcoholics, and to practice these principles in all our affairs.

## THE 12 TRADITIONS OF ALCOHOLICS ANONYMOUS

1. Our common welfare should come first; personal recovery depends upon AA unity.

2. For our group purpose there is but one ultimate authority—a loving God as He may express Himself through our group conscience. Our leaders are but trusted servants; they do not govern.

3. The only requirement for AA membership is a desire to stop drinking.

4. Each group should be autonomous except in matters affecting other groups or AA as a whole.

5. Each group has but one primary purpose—to carry its message to the alcoholic who still suffers.

6. An AA group ought never endorse, finance, or lend the AA name to any related facility or outside enterprise, lest problems of money, property, and prestige divert us from our primary purpose.

7. Every AA group ought to be fully self-supporting, declining outside contributions.

8. Alcoholics Anonymous should remain forever nonprofessional, but our service centers may employ special workers.

9. AA, as such, ought never be organized; but we may create service boards or committees directly responsible to those they serve.

10. Alcoholics Anonymous has no opinion on outside issues; hence the AA name ought never be drawn into public controversy.

11. Our public relations policy is based on attraction rather than promotion; we need always maintain personal anonymity at the level of press, radio, and films.

12. Anonymity is the spiritual foundation of all our traditions, ever reminding us to place principles before personalities.

*Note:* Many other 12-step programs modeled after Alcoholics Anonymous have adapted these steps and traditions to their own needs. These adaptations have consisted of the following changes:

a. Replacing the words *alcohol* and *alcoholics* in Steps 1 and 12 and Tradition 5 with language fitting the problem each program exists to overcome.

b. Replacing the phrases "Alcoholics Anonymous" and "AA" with the names of other programs throughout the traditions.

c. Replacing the word *drinking* with language suited to the addiction that is the basis of each program in Tradition 3.

d. Some programs have replaced the phrase "press, radio, and films" with "press, radio, films, and TV" in Tradition 11.

e. Some groups have made all references to God gender-neutral by replacing the words *Him* and *His* with *God* and *God's* in Steps 3, 7, and 11 and in Tradition 2.

f. The Sex and Love Addicts Anonymous program has replaced the phrase "in all our affairs" with "in all areas of our lives" in Step 12.

# INDEX

Addiction:
  disease definition by AMA, xi, 2
  disease model of addiction, xi, 2,
      174–175
  family/marital consequences,
      16–17, 59–60, 138, 173–177
  financial consequences, 13,
      21–22, 59–60, 138,
      217–224, 238
  health consequences, 59–60, 138,
      220, 238
  legal consequences, 13, 15, 17,
      59, 138, 238
  treatment, xi
  workplace consequences, 16, 60,
      220
Addictive personality, 209–215, 218,
    232, 240
Aftercare, xi, 5, 7
Al-Anon, 173, 177, 205
Ala-Teen, 205
Alcoholics Anonymous (AA):
  availability of meetings, 4–5
  clinicians' approaches to, xi
  effectiveness, 4
  General Service Office, 23–24,
      139, 145, 151, 169
  integration into treatment, xi–xii,
      2–12
    cons of, 2–3
    pros of, 4–7
  publications:
    *Alcoholics Anonymous*, 23,
        83–84, 110, 124, 132,
        138, 150, 154, 158, 162,
        167, 170, 174–175, 202,
        238–239

*AA and the Gay/Lesbian
    Alcoholic*, 151
*AA For the Woman*, 145
*The AA Member—
    Medications and Other
    Drugs*, 23–24, 169–170,
    230
*Grapevine*, 132
*Young People and AA*,
    139
slogans, xi
Alcoholism:
  disease definition by AMA,
      xi
Amends:
  exceptions, 111
  process of making, 108–112, 115,
      205–206, 221
  risks, 15, 107, 109, 111
  willingness to make, 105–107,
      110
American Medical Association
    (AMA), xi, 2, 174–175
American Psychiatric Association
    (APA), 174–175
Anger, 15, 17, 101, 203–204
Anonymity:
  allowable self-identification by
      clients, 8–9
  mass media, 8–9
  policies, 2, 8, 10, 55
  protection in treatment, 8, 55
Antidepressants, 19, 169
Antisocial behavior, xi
Anxiety, 17, 66, 101, 167, 227–229,
    238
Anxiety disorders, 24, 228

# ABOUT THE CD-ROM

## INTRODUCTION

This appendix provides you with information on the contents of the CD that accompanies this book. For the latest and greatest information, please refer to the ReadMe file located at the root of the CD.

## SYSTEM REQUIREMENTS

- A computer with a processor running at 120 Mhz or faster
- At least 32 MB of total RAM installed on your computer; for best performance, we recommend at least 64 MB
- A CD-ROM drive

*Note:* Many popular word processing programs are capable of reading Microsoft Word for Windows files. However, users should be aware that a slight amount of formatting might be lost when using a program other than Microsoft Word.

## USING THE CD WITH WINDOWS

To install the items from the CD to your hard drive, follow these steps:

1. Insert the CD into your computer's CD-ROM drive.
2. A window appears with the following options:
   **Install:** Gives you the option to install the author-created samples from the CD-ROM.
   **Explore:** Enables you to view the contents of the CD-ROM in its directory structure.
   **Exit:** Closes the autorun window.

If you do not have autorun enabled, or if the autorun window does not appear, follow these steps to access the CD:

1. Click Start → Run.
2. In the dialog box that appears, type **d:\setup.exe**, where *d* is the letter of your CD-ROM drive. This brings up the autorun window described in the preceding set of steps.
3. Choose the desired option from the menu. (See Step 2 in the preceding list for a description of these options.)

## WHAT'S ON THE CD

The following sections provide a summary of the software and other materials you'll find on the CD.

## Content

All author-created material from the book, including forms, slides, and lesson plans if available, are in the folder named "Content."

## Applications

The following applications are on the CD:

**Adobe Acrobat Reader**
Adobe's Acrobat Reader is a freeware viewer, to allow for viewing files in the Adobe Portable Document format.

**Microsoft Word Viewer**
Microsoft Word Viewer is a freeware viewer, to allow you to view any Microsoft Word files included. The viewer however can NOT edit or make changes to the file.

**Microsoft PowerPoint Viewer**
Microsoft PowerPoint Viewer is a freeware viewer, to allow you to view any Microsoft PowerPoint files included. The viewer however can NOT edit or make changes to the file.

**OpenOffice.org**
OpenOffice.org is a free multi-platform office productivity suite. It is very similar to Microsoft Office or Lotus SmartSuite, but OpenOffice.org is absolutely free. It includes Word Processing, Spreadsheet, Presentation, and Drawing applications

able to create professional documents, newsletters, reports, and presentations. It supports most other Office software's file formats, so you should be able to edit and view any files crated using those other Office solutions.

*Shareware programs* are fully functional, trial versions of copyrighted programs. If you like particular programs, register with their authors for a nominal fee and receive licenses, enhanced versions, and technical support.

*Freeware programs* are copyrighted games, applications, and utilities that are free for personal use. Unlike shareware, these programs do not require a fee or provide technical support.

*GNU software* is governed by its own license, which is included inside the folder of the GNU product. See the GNU license for more details.

*Trial, demo, or evaluation versions* are usually limited either by time or functionality (such as being unable to save projects). Some trial versions are very sensitive to system date changes. If you alter your computer's date, the programs will "time out" and will no longer be functional.

## User Assistance

If you have trouble with the CD-ROM, please call the Wiley Product Technical Support phone number: (800) 762-2974. Outside the United States, call 1(317) 572-3994. You can also contact Wiley Product Technical Support at **http://www.wiley.com/techsupport.** Wiley Publishing will provide technical support only for installation and other general quality control items; for technical support on the applications themselves, consult the program's vendor or author.

To place additional orders or to request information about other Wiley products, please call (800) 225-5945.